Created in Pairs

Build a Loving and Lasting Marriage Using
Sunnah Guidance to Achieve Marital Bliss

SARAH GULFRAZ

Dedication

~ Bismillah ~

May Allah (swt) accept our efforts and grant us success in this life and the next. Ameen.

In dedication to my loving family and all their support.

Contents

1. Introduction   1

2. Introduction to Islamic Marriage   4

3. Preparing for Marriage: The Islamic Approach   14

4. Islamic Marriage Contract (Nikah)   24

5. The Wedding Ceremony: Sunnah Practices   38

6. Rights & Responsibilities of Spouses   47

7. Building a Strong Foundation: Love and Mercy in Marriage   63

8. Intimacy and Sexual Ethics in Islam   71

9. Financial Management and Household Responsibilities   81

10. Parenting and Family Life in Islam   87

11. Resolving Marital Issues: Seeking Guidance from Islam   99

12. Conclusion   109

Find Out More   110

Chapter One

Introduction

I slamic teachings hold that marriage is fundamental to human existence. As the most noble creatures of Allah's (SWT) creations, humans are the masters endowed with reason and responsibilities that separate them from all other creatures. At the centre of creation are people. They have to procreate to survive, but only in compliance with the natural laws of marriage. Allah (SWT) gave people the natural desire to gravitate towards one another and draw people closer to find solace in each other.

Islam regards marriage as an act that is sacredly intertwined and ordered by Allah (SWT), which fulfils the natural human need for love and relationships. It is in no way a contract but an alliance in which the spiritual, emotional, and physical needs of both spouses are satisfied.

Humanity is perpetuated through marriage; without it, the species will go extinct. Islam sought to make this drive holy and use it to draw people closer to Allah (SWT), not leave it to be indulged in the same way as animals. So, Allah (SWT) established the institution of marriage to accomplish this.

Allah (SWT) says in Quran: "And of His signs is that He created for you from yourselves mates that you may find tranquility in them; and He placed between you affec-

tion and mercy. Indeed, in that are signs for a people who give thought?" (Quran 30:21)

The only path to a happy, healthy family is through marriage. It is the natural means of procreation and human preservation, the sole acceptable relationship between men and women, and the guardian of half of a person's faith since his wishes would be granted within the bounds Allah (SWT) had approved.

Additionally, Islam elevated matrimony from a bond of honour to a tremendous holy compact that only Islam can surpass in terms of honour.

The Islamic concept of marriage, therefore, springs from the assumption that men and women are supposed to complement each other, enhancing the strengths each brings to the partnership. A bond of such nature, when approached with true love, commitment to the Prophet Muhammad's (PBUH) teachings, and a commitment of true devotion, can indeed offer much in the way of spiritual and personal fulfilment.

But getting there and staying in a happy marriage is not without its challenges. Even the most committed relations sometimes develop conflicts and misunderstandings and have a tough time. In Islam, marriage has been considered a dynamic and ongoing journey that calls for continuous care and thoughtful effort rather than a static condition.

Allah (SWT) says: "And we have created everything in pairs that perhaps you may remember." (Quran 51:49)

"And we created you in pairs" refers to the fact that Allah (SWT) made both males and females of the same type so that they might comfort one another and show compassion and affection, which would lead to progeny.

The institution of marriage serves as a powerful weapon against the enemies of Allah (SWT) and is responsible for the profusion of the Muslim community, which will bring the Chief of the Messengers to glory alongside the other prophets on the Day of Resurrection. How fitting that one should research its events, uphold its revered customs and manners, elucidate its goals and objectives, and go into detail regarding the subject's paragraphs and chapters.

The concepts you will read in this book will lead you to a nurturing, harmonious, and long-lasting marriage whether you are planning your wedding, already married, or looking to revive and strengthen an already-existing relationship.

This book covers essential aspects of Islamic marriage according to the Sunnah, providing practical guidance and spiritual insights for couples preparing for marriage or seeking to strengthen their marital relationships. Each chapter emphasises the importance of following the example of Prophet Muhammad (PBUH) and adhering to Islamic principles in navigating the journey of marriage.

Let's dive in!

Chapter Two

Introduction to Islamic Marriage

Importance of Marriage in Islam

A contract that legally unites a man and a woman with the intention of starting a family and building a joint life is called a marriage. The Quran refers to marriage as *Mithaq Ghalith*, which translates to "a strong covenant," according to Allah (SWT).

> *"And we have taken a strong pledge (Mithaq Ghalith) from you?" (Quran 4:21)*

In Arabic, *Zawaj*, which means association and joining together, is another word for marriage. The Holy Quran uses this phrase to refer to gathering or being together in the same way. Furthermore, the definition of *Nikah*, or marriage, is "a purposeful contract to gain and keep enjoyment." It also represents the idea of gathering or assembling.

The fact that marriage offers a stable atmosphere for the preservation of amicable relationships and reciprocal love among the spouses makes it clear how valuable and important it is. It helps one maintain chastity and protect oneself from engaging in forbidden behaviours.

In a similar vein, it represents a positive method of preserving, expanding, and reproducing the family tree. As a result, Islam specifies a number of requirements that are essential or significant for a Muslim marriage to be deemed lawful, including the offer and acceptance (*Ijab wa qabul*), Wali, or a guardian for marriage, and *Mahr*, or dowry. Islam clearly demonstrates the value of the institution of marriage.

Islam views marriage as a deep spiritual bond intended to promote love, mercy, and peace between two individuals rather than merely as a social contract. Matrimony is regarded as a religious ceremony that satisfies individual and group duties.

Benefits of Marriage in Islam

Islam's view on the spiritual significance of marriage: Islam views marriage as a religious act, a chance for a couple to become closer to Allah (SWT) via their combined commitment and love. Allah (SWT) says that there is peace, love, and mercy in a married relationship.

Islam holds that the purpose of marriage is to bring comfort and tranquillity to the soul. It is a relationship in which husband and wife can strengthen their bond with Allah (SWT) and encourage one another while they carry out their religious obligations. The Prophet Muhammad (PBUH) also underlined how crucial marriage is to a Muslim's fulfilment of their faith:

> *"When a man marries, he has fulfilled half of his religion, so let him fear Allah (SWT) regarding the remaining half." (Mishkat al-Masabih)*

Using matrimony as a defence against temptation: According to Islam, marriage is an important defence against immoral behaviour. Moreover, marital bliss offers a legal and moral means of satisfying one's wishes while adhering to moral principles in a world full of detours and temptations; the optimum setting for upholding chastity is provided by marriage, as advised by the Quran:

> *"O young men, whoever among you can afford to marry, let him marry, for it helps lower the gaze and guard one's chastity." (Sunah an-Nasai)*

Muslims can safeguard themselves against temptation and make sure that their wants are satisfied in a way that pleases Allah (SWT) by getting married.

Social and emotional satisfaction: A marriage's emotional assistance and companionship are among the main reasons marriage is important in Islam. Marriage is about building a relationship built on mutual love, respect, and understanding, not only about achieving personal goals. A husband and wife should have a compassionate and friendly relationship in which they help each other through life's ups and downs.

> *Husbands are urged by the Prophet Muhammad (PBUH) to show their spouses the highest regard and consideration: "The best of you are those who are best to their wives." (Tirmidhi)*

This hadith illustrates how crucial patience and kindness are in a marriage. These pillars support a happy marriage by making both parties feel safe and cherished. This link fosters emotional and spiritual fulfilment for both spouses, which in turn fosters a calm and loving environment.

Islamic marriage creates a solid social structure and aids in preventing loneliness. Islam is a faith that places a high value on marriage as the basis for creating a secure and peaceful home.

Using marriage to strengthen the Muslim community: Marriage has a profound effect on the Muslim community as a whole, not simply the individuals involved. Strong families support strong marriages, which in turn support the development of strong societies. Islam promotes marriage to highlight the value of social stability and guaranteeing the welfare of upcoming generations. The following are some advantages of marriage according to the Prophet Muhammad (PBUH):

"Marry, for I will boast of your great numbers before other nations on the Day of Resurrection." (Sunah Ibn Majah)

Islam encourages the establishment of families and marriage, which helps the Muslim community grow and ensures that its teachings and values are passed down to the next generation.

Matrimony as a route to individual development: Islam strongly emphasises spiritual and emotional development in addition to meeting material requirements. The difficulties and obligations that accompany matrimony aid in the growth of traits like humility, patience, and compassion. By cooperating to overcome obstacles, both spouses can become better versions of themselves and deepen their relationship with Allah (SWT).

Believers were reminded of the significance of this personal development by the Prophet Muhammad (PBUH): "The believers, in their love, mercy, and kindness toward each other, are like one body; when any part of it is in pain, the rest of the body feels it and shares in the pain." (Sahih Muslim)

Quranic Verses and Hadiths Emphasising the Virtues of Marriage

The importance, benefits, and qualities of marriage are outlined in the Quran and Hadith and also direct how to maintain a morally right and loving marriage. Some of the key hadiths and verses of the Quran are mentioned below, which point toward the significance of marriage:

> *"They are clothing for you and you are clothing for them." (Quran 2:187)*

> *"And marry those among you who are single and the righteous among your male slaves and female slaves. If they are poor, Allah (SWT) will enrich them out of His bounty. And Allah (SWT) is All-Sufficient for His creatures' needs, All-Knowing." (Quran 24:32)*

> *The Prophet Muhammad (PBUH) said: "Marriage is part of my Sunnah, and whoever does not follow my Sunnah has nothing to do with me. Get married, for I will boast of your great numbers before the other nations on the Day of Judgment." (Ibn Majah)*

Wedlock in Islam is considered a source of spiritual growth, mutual support, and the completion of half of one's religious obligations. The Quran and Hadith establish this concept of marriage through explicit directions toward marital harmony, love, and respect, qualities that portray the great virtues of patience, kindness, and righteousness.

Purpose of Marriage From an Islamic Perspective

There are several reasons why marriage is a significant institution. To guarantee the survival of the human race and the preservation of the human species, Allah (SWT) stated as much to the Muslim community.

> *"O mankind! Be mindful of your Lord, Who created you from a single soul and from it, He created its mate; and from them has spread abroad a multitude of men and women" (Quran 4:1)*

In addition to upholding Islam, marriage allows a Muslim to enjoy worldly satisfaction. Happiness and faith are significant facets of a person's psyche.

Human character is cultivated via marriage by giving a man a sense of accountability and equipping him to fulfil his roles as a husband and a father. Likewise, matrimony imbues a woman with a sense of obligation as a spouse and mother. Sadly, some people steer clear of marriage because of their skewed perceptions and inclination to avoid taking on responsibilities and living like adults without a home, responsibilities, or meaningful relationships.

They prove to be worthless and lose their value in the pursuit of a meaningful existence. All of these are the result of a lack of understanding of the importance of marriage, which symbolises a strong commitment and shared responsibility.

> *"Men are the guardians of women because Allah has made men-some of them-to excel the other, for, they spend of their property (for the support of women). So good women are those women who are obedient and guard in secret what Allah has guarded." (Quran 4:34)*

As a result, Islam specifies explicitly the duties that a husband has to his spouse, including providing for her safety, refraining from using derogatory words and providing for her material needs, among other things. In addition, the wife has other duties to her husband, such as showing him love and tolerance, refraining from filing for divorce without a good reason and carrying out other duties prescribed by the Quran and the Prophet's (PBUH) tradition. Therefore, each husband and wife must bear accountability for all these duties.

The only institution for starting a family is marriage. The family is the fundamental unit of the societal framework and is necessary for the existence of any acceptable human society. Family is the setting in which intimate relationships, such as those between parents and children, siblings, and mothers, emerge. These relationships also instil a sincere feeling of love and compassion, selflessness, kindness, concern, and collaboration in a Muslim.

Married individuals can better concentrate on their work since they have someone to look after them and their children, which motivates them to accomplish their jobs professionally.

A married man can, therefore, perform his duties correctly, effectively, and with great satisfaction when he is at ease. On the other hand, an unmarried man's thinking is disorganised rather than focused. He may be worried about his job, house, and the weight of making ends meet and buying clothes; essentially, his mind is consumed.

Islamic Principles of Marital Relationships

Based on love, responsibility, respect, and compassion for the other, principles of love represent the foundation on which Islamic marriage customs are built. Guidelines for building a good and peaceful marriage can be found in the Quran and the Sunnah. Some of the most important ideas are the following:

Understanding the Concept of Partnership (zawaj) in Islam

Islam interprets *zawaj* as marriage, which has its roots in both the worldly and spiritual facets of human existence. Marriage is viewed as a very important contract between two people because it creates a loving, caring, and respectful family environment. A person fulfils more fundamental spiritual and moral commitments through marriage, which is more than just a friendship bond.

Islamic marriage is a contract that requires the free consent of both spouses. The requirements included in this contract are as follows: the bride has the right to receive a Mahr, which is evidence of security for her. According to the beliefs followed by Islam, this contract is also negotiable; therefore, there is flexibility in the relationship between the spouses. Witnesses perform the Nikah, usually followed by a public ceremony to present the union and seal the couple within their community.

In Islam, zawaj is more than a legal or social arrangement—it is a deep union founded in faith, respect, and love. Both parties are entrusted with balancing their relationship, which nurtures emotional, spiritual, and practical harmony.

Marriage is a natural necessity for everyone. It has several beneficial impacts, the most important being the formation of a family, which offers security and peace of mind. A single individual resembles a bird without a nest. Marrying someone might provide solace to someone who is lost in life because a spouse is someone with whom they can share joys and sorrows. The want to have sex is strong and a fundamental emotion; everyone should have a partner to satisfy their sexual needs in a secure and comfortable environment.

Everyone has the right to a healthy and suitable sexual encounter. Individuals who opt not to marry often have mental and/or physical health problems. These illnesses, along with several social problems, are directly linked to teenage abstinence from marriage. Reproduction: Marriage is how people continue to have children. As the offspring of marriage, children are both essential to bolstering the family's foundations and a genuine source of enjoyment for their parents. Islamic customs and the Holy Quran both emphasise the importance of marriage and starting a family.

For the human race, marriage serves a different kind of purpose. It was not intended for humans to come into this world merely to live and consume, seek enjoyment, or indulge in sensual behaviour, only to perish and be destroyed. Man has a higher rank than such actions. Humans are intended to educate themselves and their souls by learning moral lessons, doing good deeds, and acting politely. Man is created to walk the straight path and become closer to the Almighty Allah (SWT).

Humanity is a creation that can purify the soul and, through abstaining from evil activities and acting morally, rise to a state that even angels cannot achieve. Humanity is an immortal creature. Man has come to this planet to ensure his pleasure, both here on Earth and in the Hereafter, through the guidance of the messengers and the application of the programs established by the religion (Islam) so that he can dwell in peace in the Hereafter for all eternity.

Living an honourable and truthful life greatly depends upon having a trustworthy, devout, and peaceful companion. A companion like this helps one stay committed to the required acts of worship and is a significant factor in avoiding evil behaviours. A devout couple supports one another and has no difficulties accomplishing their religious objectives. Just as a corrupt person would lure his spouse towards corruption, a pious person would always invite them to righteousness.

Therefore, it makes sense that Islamic men and women who wish to be married are counselled to view their potential spouse's piety and "good manners" as prerequisites.

As a result, it is important to consider marriage's purpose within this spiritual framework. For a religious individual, marriage should be an opportunity to abstain from evil activities and cleanse one's soul of sins. It should be a way to become closer to the Allah (SWT). It is within this framework that a suitable partner becomes crucial.

"If I were to bestow all the good of both worlds upon a Muslim person, I would endow him with a humble heart, a tongue which continuously utters his praises, a body patient enough to withstand all calamities; and I would give him a pious spouse who, when she sees him becomes happy, and protects his property and her own honour in his absence." (Tirmidhi)

When two believers get married and start a family, their sexual relationship will help them grow in their love and kindness for one another. In this relationship, there will not be any threats of sexual perversion, harmful addictions, or illegal acts.

"One person went to the Prophet and said: 'I have a wife who always welcomes me when I come home, and escorts me to the door when I leave. When she finds me sad and unhappy, she then, by consoling me says: If you are thinking of sustenance, then do not despair, because Allah provides sustenance; and if you are thinking about the next life, then may Allah increase your intellect and efforts. Then the Prophet stated: 'Allah surely has functionaries and agents in this world and your wife is one of those. Such a woman would be rewarded half as much as a martyr." (Sunah Ibn Majah)

Chapter Three

Preparing for Marriage: The Islamic Approach

Importance of Intention (Niyyah) and Sincerity in Seeking Marriage

In Islam, the term "intention" (*Niyyah*) describes the attitude and drive behind performing good activities to please Allah (SWT). According to Umar Ibn Al-Khattab (RA), he heard the Prophet Muhammad (PBUH) saying:

> *"Verily actions are by intentions, and for every person is what he intended. So the one whose Hijrah was to Allah and His Messenger, then his Hijrah was to Allah and His Messenger and the one whose hijrah was for the world to gain from it, or a woman to marry her, then his Hijrah was to what he made Hijrah for." (Sahih Bukhari)*

Intentions are important in Islam, not only in religious practice but in all facets of life. Muslims are urged to act with intention in mind at all times and try to carry out good activities with sincere intentions. Any action is said to begin with the idea of intention or Niyyah in Arabic.

Throughout the Quran, Allah (SWT) discusses the idea of intention and stresses the significance of acting with sincere and pure intentions.

"And not for anyone else does he spend of his wealth, but only seeking the face of his Lord, the Most High" (Quran 92:20)

In Islam, marriage is not something between a man and a woman but rather a holy contract that aims to raise mutual love, compassion, and even spiritual growth. An act of worship, like all acts of worship, must be entered into with the right intention (Niyyah) and sincerity. A person seeking marriage should ensure their heart and mind are in the light of the teachings of Islam. These will guide the believer toward ultimate success in both life and the Hereafter.

Any righteous act in Islam begins with the purification of intention. One should not search for marriage with the motives of material benefit, an excellent social standing, or lustful desires but with the right intention of pleasing Allah (SWT), as it fulfils half of a person's faith and builds up a complete household according to the values of Islam.

This is a true intention in a marriage – it transforms what might otherwise be a transaction of this world into an act of worship. A marriage born out of the desire to seek the pleasure of Allah (SWT) is a marriage that would, indeed, be blessed with Barakah. Besides, facing tests and troubles in marriage can serve as valuable lessons for spiritual development and purification of the soul. These experiences strengthen the couple, providing a solid foundation for their unity in worshipping Allah (SWT) and adhering faithfully to His words.

Being real with oneself and one's potential partner is integral to being truthful when seeking marriage. It eliminates dishonesty and hidden agendas. A sincere follower does not ask for marriage to self-serve or manipulate someone else; rather, they view this stage as the realisation of faith, a means to establish a just family loyal to Allah (SWT), and mutual support in righteousness. By adopting this mentality, a couple guarantees that their relationship will be the primary foundation for their shared love for their Creator.

Qualities to Look for in a Spouse Based on Islamic Teachings

Selecting a spouse is one of the most significant decisions a person will ever make. Our family is unavoidable, but we do have a choice in which we choose to raise as a family. We are allowed to marry whomever we like, provided that it complies with Islamic law, thanks to Allah (SWT).

Finding a spouse in Islam requires navigation through the process to guarantee that it is undertaken in accordance with Islamic principles. Thus, the foundation of this marriage is love, respect for one another, and religion. This essay offers guidance on how to carry out this significant journey in accordance with Islamic beliefs.

Characteristics of an Ideal Wife

In Islam, an ideal wife's attributes extend beyond her physical attributes and financial status. Rather, piety, morality, integrity, and kindness are emphasised. When choosing a partner, the Prophet Muhammad (PBUH) counselled, giving priority to moral character and religious commitment. The teachings of the Quran emphasise these characteristics as being crucial when deciding who would make the best spouse.

- **Looking for a single woman**

Islam promotes the pursuit of unmarried women, including widows, divorcees, and virgins. If one has the option, experts advise marrying a virgin; nonetheless, it is also considered beneficial to marry widows and divorced women.

The Quran says: "Marry those among you who are single." (Quran 24:32)

• **Importance of choosing the right partner**

Choosing a spouse who positively contributes to personal growth and aids in achieving success in this life and the Hereafter is vital.

The Prophet Muhammad (PBUH) emphasised: "Choose carefully for your seed, for verily women give birth to children resembling their brothers and sisters." (Sunah Ibn Majah)

• **The four qualities to consider**

Islam advises men to marry women based on four criteria: wealth, family status, beauty, and religious devotion.

The Prophet (PBUH) said, "Marry a woman for four things: her wealth, family status, beauty, and religious commitment. Marry the one who is religious, or you will lose out." (Sahih Al-Bukhari)

• **Poverty should not be a barrier**

While wealth is acknowledged in relationships, piety takes precedence. If a prospective spouse possesses the qualities of faith and good character, financial constraints should not deter the union. The Quran and Hadith repeatedly affirm that marrying even in a state of poverty will bring blessings, as Allah (SWT) enriches those who trust in Him.

• **Choosing a woman who can bear children**

Marrying a woman capable of bearing children is highly encouraged, as it contributes to the upbringing of future generations. The Prophet (PBUH) advised marrying women who love and are fertile, stating, "I will take pride in your great numbers on the Day of Judgment." It is essential to consider both the physical and emotional qualities that enable a woman to fulfil the nurturing role in the family.

- **Faith as a key factor**

Islam emphasises the importance of a woman's religious devotion over beauty or wealth. The Prophet (PBUH) advised against marrying for superficial reasons, stating that a woman's commitment to faith is the most valuable quality in a partner. Marrying for religious compatibility ensures a stronger foundation for the marriage.

- **Marrying divorced women**

While it is recommended to marry a virgin when given the choice, the Prophet Muhammad (PBUH) recognised the rewards of marrying widows or divorced women. He compared caring for such individuals to participating in noble acts of worship, highlighting the virtues of compassion and service.

Qualities of a Good Married Man

Islamic teachings provide clear guidance on what to look for in a potential husband. Key considerations are a man's ability to fulfil the responsibilities of marriage, his character, and his religious devotion.

- **Financial and physical readiness**

The Prophet (PBUH) encouraged young men who could afford to marry to do so, as marriage helps to protect them from immoral behaviour. Affordability refers to the ability to provide for a wife financially and engage in marital relations.

- **Strong moral character**

Good character is crucial when choosing a spouse. A man who demonstrates honesty, kindness, respect, and empathy is essential for a stable and healthy marriage. A virtuous character fosters a relationship built on trust and mutual respect.

- **Fear of Allah (SWT) and Respectfulness**

A potential husband's fear of Allah (SWT) is a core quality that guides him to treat his wife with dignity and care.

The Prophet (PBUH) said, "Fear Allah (SWT) in your treatment of women, for you have taken them with the trust of Allah (SWT)" (Sahih Muslim)

- **Demonstrating justice and kindness**

Justice and kindness in interactions, especially with one's spouse, are fundamental to a successful marriage. The husband is encouraged to provide for his wife's needs and resolve disputes fairly.

Finding a spouse in Islam is a significant step that requires patience, sincerity, and reliance on Allah (SWT). The process should prioritise qualities like piety, good character, and compatibility. Open communication with family and trusted mentors can also be helpful. With trust in Allah's (SWT) plan and adherence to Islamic principles, the journey toward finding a spouse can be approached with faith and optimism.

Steps to Spiritually Prepare for Marriage According to the Sunnah

Islamic custom holds that getting married should be done for Allah's (SWT) sake. Thus, marriage is Ibadah (worship). Seeking direction from Allah (SWT) on all issues is important, especially when deciding who to marry and when to get married. Similarly, we need to pray to Allah (SWT) to get us through difficult times.

Islamic custom states that studying religious customs and practices is a part of preparing a believer for marriage. This helps the believer understand Islam in all its dimensions, including marriage.

Preparing spiritually before committing to the holy bond of marriage is necessary. To start, one must cleanse one's heart and reaffirm one's intentions for Allah's sake (SWT). It is important to consider the reasons behind marriage and ensure that seeking Allah's (SWT) pleasure is the main objective. This entails pleading with Allah (SWT) to direct one's steps, grant clarity, and bestow piety and peace on the union.

> *Allah (SWT) says: "And your Lord said: Invoke Me (believe in Me alone and ask Me anything) I will respond to your (invocation). Verily, those who scorn My worship (i.e., they do not believe in My Oneness or ask Me), they will surely enter hell in humiliation" (Quran 40:60)*

If Istikhara is carried out with sincerity, seeking Allah's (SWT) guidance in selecting a match, a marriage will be built on the strongest possible foundation from the start. The best models of proper Islamic behaviour in family life can be found in the Holy Quran and the Prophet's Sunnah, both of which are filled with knowledge.

Individuals looking to get married must consider the guidance provided by Allah (SWT) and His Messenger. In choosing a partner, one should also follow the Prophet Muhammad's (PBUH) custom of praying the Istikhara (decision-making) prayer, which asks Allah (SWT) to guide one in choosing the mate who will best help one preserve their *Iman* (faith) to get ready for the Ahkirah (life after death).

Another important preparation is to seek knowledge. Islam emphasises the importance of education, which applies to the knowledge of marital responsibilities and rights. Both men and women should study the rights of their future spouses as outlined in the Quran and Sunnah. Understanding these roles helps to establish clear expectations within the marriage and prevents potential disputes. Seeking advice from righteous scholars or mentors is another critical step.

"The religion is sincere advice." (Sahih Muslim)

Consulting those who have experience and wisdom can help clarify doubts and provide practical insights into navigating the marital journey in a way that is pleasing to Allah (SWT).

Marriage in Islam is a profound act of worship that requires pure intention, sincerity, and spiritual preparation. By seeking a spouse with piety, good character, and a shared commitment to Islamic principles, one can establish a relationship that is blessed and enduring. Through regular worship, seeking knowledge, and aligning one's intentions with the teachings of Islam, both husband and wife can journey together on the path to attaining the pleasure of Allah (SWT) and the ultimate reward in the Hereafter.

The Role of Families in Islamic Marriages

Families, particularly parents and guardians, play a crucial and fundamental role in Islamic marriages. Islam places a strong emphasis on the family, and these families are a reflection of how much the religion values social cohesion, accountability, and respect. Marriage unites two families and strengthens the bonds between the partners. This link highlights the need for all marriage-related decisions to be made with consideration for family relationships and in line with Islamic beliefs and values.

Involvement of Parents and Guardians in the Marriage Process

In Islam, parents and guardians take part in the marriage process, often making their involvement a compulsory step, particularly for women. The guardian, or wali, is held responsible for ensuring that the marriage is conducted according to Islamic law.

"There is no marriage except with a wali." (Sunan Abu Dawood)

This verse underscores the importance of this role in protecting a woman's rights and ensuring the marriage proposal is fair, reasonable, and in accordance with Islamic law.

Parents and guardians are invaluable in this regard, as their experience in life, wisdom, and insight help guide their children in more sound decisions. They determine whether or not a spouse is suitable according to the Islamic qualifications of a prospective mate: piety, character, and so much more. More often than not, the interference helps prevent rash or ill-conceived decisions that ensure that the marriage is founded on a strong basis.

The wali is a Muslim male who acts on behalf of the woman in matters of marriage. His role is to help her select a suitable husband and ensure the marriage aligns with Islamic principles. The wali is typically the woman's father; if unavailable, the role passes to the closest male relative, such as the grandfather, brother, or uncle. According to the majority of Islamic scholars, a marriage without the wali is considered invalid, based on several hadiths emphasising the necessity of a guardian.

The wali must be of the same religion as the woman. For example, a non-Muslim father cannot serve as the wali for a Muslim daughter. The wali's primary duty is to choose a suitable husband based on religious compatibility and character rather than personal preferences or biases. If a qualified suitor is rejected by the wali for reasons not supported by Islamic principles, the woman has the right to seek intervention from a judge, who can override the wali's decision. In conclusion, the wali serves as a protective figure who upholds Islamic principles during the marriage process, ensuring the woman's rights are respected and that the marriage is conducted appropriately.

In most cultures, the primary process of engagement or acceptance is with the parents, so it is established that both families get along and that this union will help to develop mutual respect and cooperation. In contrast, while Islam does indeed encourage the involvement of parents, it does respect the individual right to choose a spouse.

The Prophet emphasised the importance of mutual consent in marriage, and any coercion or force is strictly prohibited in Islam. It is narrated that a woman came to the Prophet and said, "My father has married me off without my consent," and the Prophet gave her the choice to annul the marriage (Sunah Ibn Majah)

This highlights the balance between the role of guardians in protecting their children and the individual's right to make their own decisions.

Of course, parents can also provide emotional support to their children during the marriage process. The dua, or blessings bestowed upon them, are highly desired. In Islam, parents' prayers for their children have a certain power. The Prophet (PBUH) also emphasised treating parents with compassion and respect and that receiving their blessings and prayers strengthens the relationship between families and couples.

Hence, the role of families, especially parents, in Islamic marriages is profound, rooted in the principles of mutual respect, cooperation, and adherence to Islamic values. The involvement of parents and guardians in the marriage process ensures that the union is based on sound religious principles, while family support during marriage preparations helps maintain harmony and ease the transition into married life.

By working together with sincerity and humility, families can play a vital role in ensuring the success and longevity of the marriage, helping the couple build a strong, faith-centered partnership.

Chapter Four

Islamic Marriage Contract (Nikah)

Significance of the Marriage Contract in Islam

I slamic marriage is a sacred relationship with significant religious and ethical ramifications, not merely a social or personal arrangement. It is established on the basis of the Islamic marriage contract, known as Nikah.

The Nikah, by defining respective rights, obligations, and responsibilities as prescribed by the Quran and Sunnah, represents the commitment between husband and wife. It symbolises the gravity of marriage's obligation in Allah's (SWT) eyes and its seriousness as an act of worship.

> *"O mankind! We have created you from a male and a female, and made you into nations and tribes, that you may know one another. Verily, the most honourable of you with Allah (SWT) is that believer who has At-Taqwa (Piety)." (Quran 49:13)*

"Allah (SWT), it is He who has made for you the earth as a dwelling place and the sky as a canopy, and has given you shape (form) and made your shapes good looking..." (Quran 49:64)

"He created the heavens and the earth, and He shaped you and made good your shapes, and to Him is the final return." (Quran 64:3)

The text does not assert that Adam was formed androgynous, as the Gnostic magi do, nor does it say, "We produced you from part-male and part-female." Authentic gender identity, as perfectly decreed and produced by Al'Mussawwir, the Bestower of Form, is devoid of ambiguity or dualism.

The verses suggest that the first marriage was rooted in Divine love, with *At-Taqwa* (piety) present from the start of the marriage and subsequently passed down through generations. This romance, created by Allah (SWT) between the idealised Adam and Eve – both idealised male and female forms and also perfectly "good-looking shapes" – served as a model of human submission, trust, and faith in our Creator. This divinely guided union symbolises our purpose beyond pain, death, and annihilation.

The legal act of marriage is known as Nikah, which is another word for *Aqd*, which means to bond together. Divorce is the act of Talaq, which translates to breaking free from marriage. *Mutlaq*, which we use in Urdu to denote "totally," also refers to freedom. *Nisaa* is the Arabic term for woman. However, the Arabic term for marriage is Nikah, derived from the root *Nkh*, which means thoroughly combining.

The Islamic marriage contract has proper guidelines and basic rules about marriage according to Islamic teachings and boundaries. When to marry? The appropriate age and time to get married is when a person reaches both sexual and mental maturity. The ability to create a friendly home environment and uphold family members' rights may be indicators of mental maturity. The need for a mate and family is an innate human need that Allah (SWT), in His wisdom, has implanted in humanity.

This need arises at the appropriate time and season and must be met. If it is responded to promptly and meets its requirements, it follows its natural path and renders the individual flawless. If it is answered incorrectly or in an unnatural way or if it is delayed, it veers off course, rebels, and becomes corrupt not only in itself but also in man.

Islam outlines various instructions for a man to follow to be qualified to take a woman's hand in marriage. In line with Islamic law, a boy is considered *Baligh*, or to have reached puberty, when he becomes fifteen or reaches sexual maturity. However, this is insufficient to sign a marriage contract. In addition to the regulations pertaining to puberty, *Rushd* is a notion that means "capability of sensible conduct" or maturity. A husband must be Rashid, and a wife must be Rashidah to carry out the duties of marriage properly.

What You Must Understand

Since marriage is a legally binding contract that outlines the obligations and rights of each party, it connects not only two people but also their separate families. Here, we'll examine the nuances of the Muslim marriage contract and offer helpful guidance for those seeking to comprehend and navigate this procedure.

The Islamic matrimonial contract is a holy pact between two people and their families. It is a legally binding agreement that delineates the respective rights and obligations of all parties involved and is revered in the Muslim faith. The contract has multiple important elements and is usually carried out before an Islamic cleric.

These consist of the exchange of vows, the dowry presentation, and the bride's consent statement. At least two adult Muslims typically witness the contract, serving as witnesses to the terms of the pact.

It is significant to remember that the Muslim marriage agreement has legal ramifications in addition to being a religious or cultural ritual. In order for it to be enforceable, the contract must be published with the government in certain nations where the overwhelming population is Muslim. The Muslim marriage contract has religious and cultural significance for both parties and their families, even though it is not legally recognised by the government in other nations.

The Prophet Muhammad (PBUH) said: "No house has been built in Islam more beloved in the sight of Allah (SWT) than through marriage." (Sunah Ibn Majah)

Moreover, the Prophet (PBUH) stated, "The best people of my nation (Ummah) are those who get married, and the worst people of my nation are those who avoid marriage and live as bachelors." (Kanz al-Ummal)

The *Nikah* assumes a significant position in Islamic law because it elevates the state of the relationship between man and woman from purely one of companionship to that of an important partnership ordained by God. The *Nikah* formalises the bond to ground it on mutual respect, love, and the pursuit of a common spiritual journey.

The Islamic marriage contract

The proposal known as an *Ijab* or *Rishta* is the first step in the most typical Islamic marriage. In traditional Islamic jurisprudence, a formal proposal is not mandatory but is usually observed. After being accepted, the engaged pair gets a chance to get to know one another. The fiancés can see one another, talk, interact with relatives, and assess their compatibility in a chaperoned setting.

The next step is to sign the Islamic marriage contract in an official ceremony called Nikah. In traditional Islamic jurisprudence, the marriage contract solemnises the physical connection between a man and woman and serves as the foundation for their marriage. By signing the Islamic marriage contract, couples commit to nurturing an environment of love and mercy that is conducive to Islamic growth; it is considered to be a sacred covenant involving two consenting (Qabool) parties making an agreement in the presence of two witnesses.

The other schools of Islamic law regard fathers as their daughters' principal Walis, with grandfathers, siblings, or the next eligible male relative coming in second. According to conventional Islamic law, men who wish to marry women portrayed by Walis must first ask the guardian for permission to wed their daughter or another female relative. The Wali then asks the bride if she approves of the marriage.

Islamic custom dictates that husbands give their spouses a *Mahr* or wedding present (Quran 4:20). The Mahr can be provided in any sum, from cash to gold to real estate, with no set minimum or maximum. The Mahr becomes the bride's property, to be used whatever she pleases, and an additional source of safety and support.

As long as they are able, males are required under traditional Islamic law to support their wives financially in the same way that they used to live. The Mahr is payable upon request, divorce, or the husband's passing. It can be provided at the beginning of the marriage, during the marriage, or split into immediate and postponed instalments.

If the wife chooses to work during the marriage, her earnings become her distinct marital property, and she is under no duty to provide for the family's needs financially. Additionally, caring for any infants and doing housework is optional but paid.

Typical provisions tend to protect women's rights by helping couples agree with an equal right to file for divorce, an agreement to stay monogamous, the right to work and education, and an equal division of domestic duties and living conditions. However, the legal rights of women vary among Muslim countries.

To put it briefly, the most typical Islamic marriage consists of an offer, acceptance, public marriage announcement, and marriage contract signing in front of two witnesses. Islamic law, in its traditional form, mandates that a husband provide for his wife financially. Should the spouse decide to work, her income will be considered her own independent marital property.

One of the main reasons Nikah is insisted upon is its protection of the rights and interests of the partners. It is a legal declaration of a couple's responsibility toward each other and thus ensures that the union is based on equity and justice. By entering into the Nikah, both individuals commit to upholding the principles of kindness, equality, and fidelity, as instructed in the Quran:

> *"Live with them in kindness; even if you dislike them, perhaps you dislike something in which Allah (SWT) has placed much good" (Quran 4:19)*

This makes the Nikah a significant act of devotion to Allah (SWT), as it aligns the couple's intentions with His divine will.

Legal and Ethical Aspects of the Nikah Ceremony

Besides the conditions for the validity of Nikah, significant ethical and legal considerations are included in the ceremony itself. The Nikah is required to be conducted modestly, simply, and in the manner of Islam so that it is a dignified and respectful affair, as ensured by the Islamic call for conducting this important matter. The legality secured through the Nikah protects both spouses' rights as the ethical considerations promote compassion, mutual respect, and responsibility.

From a legal standpoint, the Nikah formalises the rights and responsibilities of a spouse that represent the right to companionship, financial support, and protection from harm. The male partner is bound to provide for his wife's material needs, including food, shelter, and clothing, as guided clearly in the Quran:

"Men are the protectors and maintainers of women"
(Quran 4:34)

The wife also has an obligation to respect her husband and manage the household with wisdom and care.

The Nikah contract also legally protects both the husband and wife in case their rights are breached. For example, if one of the spouses refuses to fulfil their obligations, Islamic law provides a way to solve the problem: mediation or, in extreme cases, divorce. On the other hand, Islam strongly forbids divorce unless necessary and encourages couples to bear patiently and understand their problems.

The ethical dimension of the Nikah ceremony is rooted in the Quran's guidance on maintaining a marriage based on love, mercy, and kindness.

The Messenger of Allah (PBUH) said: "The best of you are those who are best to their families." (Sunan Ibn Majah)

This hadith reminds both spouses of the importance of treating one another with compassion and fairness.

Islam also encourages simplicity in marriage ceremonies. The Prophet (PBUH) recommended that weddings be modest affairs, free from extravagance and showiness.

He said, "The best of marriages are those that are the easiest" (Sunan Ibn Majah)

By keeping the Nikah simple and within one's means, the focus remains on the sacred nature of the union rather than worldly displays of wealth or status.

For example, in the Nikah, the couple invites Allah's (SWT) blessings. It is reported that prophets would recite dua together after Nikah to seek Allah's (SWT) blessings for their union, fostering a peaceful marriage. This adds a spiritual dimension to the ceremony, reminding the couple that the marriage represents a path to pleasing Allah (SWT) and earning rewards here and Hereafter.

The Nikah is much more than the formality of tying the knot; it is built on far, far more sacred bonds that create a covenant, and it reverberates with the sanctity of marriage in Islam. With a valid Nikah, in understanding its components and conditions, the husband and wife are ready to take on their lives in mutual support, love, and respect - seeking Allah's (SWT) pleasure at each step of their marriage.

With Whom Nikah is Haram?

- **Father-in-law and paternal ancestors**: A woman cannot marry her father-in-law or his father or grandfather.

- **Close blood relatives:** Marriage with one's brothers, uncles, and nephews is not allowed. A brother is considered someone with either the same parents, a shared father but a different mother, or a shared mother but a different father. If both parents are different, the person is not considered a brother, and marriage is valid.

- **Marriage between sisters of the same husband:** If two sisters marry the same person, the marriage of the sister who was married first will be considered valid, while the second marriage will not.

- **Direct descendants and ascendants:** Marriage with one's children, grandchildren, great-grandchildren, parents, grandparents, or maternal grandparents is not permissible.

- **Marrying a fifth wife:** If a man has four wives, he cannot marry a fifth. If he divorces one of the four, a new marriage is not allowed until the divorced wife's waiting period (iddah) is completed.

- **Marriage between two closely related women:** If two women are closely related, they cannot be married to the same person at the same time; their marriage would be invalid. A second marriage to one of them is only permissible if the first wife either passes away or is divorced and completes her waiting period (iddah).

- **Marriage to son-in-law:** Marrying one's son-in-law is forbidden in all circumstances, regardless of whether the daughter is still living with him.

- **Waiting period after divorce or death:** A woman must complete her waiting period (iddah) after divorce or her husband's death before remarrying.

- **Marriage to stepfather:** A girl can only marry her stepfather if her mother did not live with him before her passing or divorce.

- **Marriage to stepchildren:** Marrying one's stepchildren is prohibited. For example, if a man has several wives, none of them can marry the children of the other wives, regardless of whether they lived with the stepparent.

- **Marriage with a non-Muslim**: A Muslim woman is not permitted to marry a man who follows a different religion; she can only marry a Muslim.

- **Improper intentions**: If a boy touches his stepmother with bad intentions, she becomes prohibited from her husband, and there is no way for her to become permissible for him again. The same rule applies if the stepmother touches her stepson with bad intentions.

- **Marriage after inappropriate contact**: If a woman or man touches a non-related individual with inappropriate intentions, that person's mother or children become prohibited from marriage.

- **Accidental intimacy**: If a man mistakenly touches his daughter or mother-in-law with the passions of youth, believing them to be his wife, he becomes permanently forbidden from his wife.

- **Cousins and distant relatives**: Two women who are not sisters by blood but are cousins on either their mother's or father's side can marry the same man at the same time. Similarly, if a distant aunt is involved, she and her niece can marry the same man simultaneously.

- **Breastfeeding relations:** All prohibitions regarding marriage due to blood relations also apply to relationships formed through breastfeeding. If a particular woman breastfed a girl, that girl cannot marry the woman's husband or children, as they are considered her family.

- **Adopted children**: Since adoption is not recognised in Islamic law, an adopted son does not become a biological son, so it is permissible to marry one's adopted child.

- **Marriage of stepmother and stepdaughter to the same man**: If a woman and her stepdaughter marry the same person, the marriage will be valid.

- **Pregnancy due to adultery**: If a woman is not married but becomes pregnant due to adultery, marriage is allowed, but they cannot be intimate until after the child is born. However, if she marries the father of the child, intercourse is permissible.

- **Marriage with aunts or nieces**: A husband cannot marry his wife's aunts or nieces while he is married to her.

- **Breastfed sisters:** If two sisters have been breastfed by the same woman, they cannot marry the same man at the same time.

- **Sunni-Shia marriages**: Marriage between a Sunni girl and a Shia man is considered impermissible by most scholars.

- **Marriage to distant uncles**: If a man has a distant family relationship that makes him a non-biological uncle, marriage to him is permissible. Likewise, marrying a distant paternal uncle or nephew is also allowed, as is marriage to cousins.

- **Stepmother's husband as potential spouse**: A girl may marry her stepfather if her mother did not live with him before passing away or divorce.

- **Brother-in-law**: A woman cannot marry her brother-in-law while her sister is still married to him. However, if her sister passes away or is divorced and the waiting period is completed, then the marriage is permissible.

- **Adultery prohibitions:** If a man commits adultery with a woman, he cannot marry her mother or children.

- **Marriage to adopted son:** Marriage with an adopted son is permissible since adoption does not make him a biological child.

Mahr (Dowry) in Islamic marriages

In the Islamic tradition, *mahr* is an essential component of the marriage contract (Nikah), symbolising the respect, responsibility, and commitment that the groom offers to the bride. The mahr is a mandatory gift from the groom to the bride, which becomes her exclusive property. Its significance is deeply rooted in Islamic teachings. It provides financial security for the bride while emphasising the groom's duty to honour and care for his spouse.

Who takes Mahr?

The wife's mahr is her property, and no one, not even her parents, may take any of it without her consent. Some may dispute the foregoing by mentioning the tale of the elderly man who proposed marriage to Hazrat Musa (AS) and then demanded labour from the latter as her dowry. While this may have been legal under pre-Islamic regulations, it was outlawed under Islam. Moreover, it is possible that Hazrat Musa's (AS) wife benefited from his assistance to her father, or that she chose to give up her mahr as a gift to her father, or perhaps they had an agreement where she received something in return for Hazrat Musa's (AS) assistance.

The mahr is a payment the woman receives from her husband as payment for her availability. So, even in the event of a divorce—that is, if her husband files for divorce without waiting for any action from her—Allah (SWT) grants her the whole right to it. Says Allah (SWT):

> *"And if you want to replace one wife with another and have given one of them a great amount [in gifts], do not take [back] from it anything. Would you take it in injustice and manifest sin? And how could you take it while you have gone in unto each other, and they have taken from you a solemn covenant?" (Quran 4:20-21)*

The verse advises men not to reclaim any part of this wealth if they choose to replace one wife with another. It highlights the principle of fairness and justice in marital relationships, indicating that even if a large amount of wealth (a qintar) has been given, it should not be taken back unjustly.

Kinds of Dowry

Money, jewellery, clothing, or other tangible items might be given as dowry. It could also be an intangible gift. The dowry should be determined by the husband's financial situation as well as what is appropriate for the bride, given her social standing. Agreement between the bride and her Wali (or husband) usually determines it.

According to Sahl Bin Sa'd (RA), a woman once approached the Prophet (PBUH) and proposed marriage to him. The Prophet (PBUH) declined and said he needed no more wives. One of the men who was with him said, "O Messenger of Allah! Wed her to me." "Do you have anything?" the Prophet (PBUH) asked him (to give her). "No," he exclaimed. "Give her an iron ring, at the at least," the Prophet (PBUH) instructed. He was still unable to pay it, though. Have you memorised any passages from the Quran, he (PBUH) asked. "I memorised such-and-such surahs," he responded.

Then the Prophet (PBUH) declared: "Go, I have married her to you for the portion of the Quran which you have memorised." (Sahih Bukhari)

It can be asked, "What benefit did she get from his memorisation of the Quran?" In response, he would be expected to treat her with kindness and impart some of the moral lessons he had learnt via his memorisation of those lessons. The bride would gain far more from all of it than expensive gifts.

Certain cultures demand the husband to make additional financial commitments to the bride, such as purchasing clothes, jewellery, and other items, in addition to the Mahr, which is a certain amount of money. To prevent future problems, it is best to explicitly identify the Mahr in the marriage contract, as all of that is considered part of it under Islamic law.

Islam does not have a maximum dowry amount, although it is advised to keep it modest and accessible to the spouse. An oppressive Mahr could portend a terrible and heartless marriage. The woman's parents often ask for very large dowries in Muslim countries. Due to this, a large number of young men have chosen to delay or completely give up on marriage, which has allowed *zina* and other vices to proliferate among the youth. As a result, the parents ought to be thoughtful and aware that putting too much pressure on the spouse damages both their daughters and the Muslim community as a whole.

> *Abu Hurayrah (RA) reported that a man came to the Prophet (PBUH) and said, "I have married a woman from al-Ansar." The Prophet (PBUH) asked him how much (Mahr) did you give her? He replied, "Four uqiyyahs." Noting his limited financial condition and that he needed help paying that Mahr, the Prophet (PBUH) said disapprovingly: "It is as if you are carving silver out of a mountain. I can give you nothing. Go and seek something, even if it is just a ring of iron." (Sunan Ibn Majah)*

This hadith reflects the Prophet's (PBUH) concern for modesty and practicality in marriage, ensuring that the Mahr is within the means of the husband without causing hardship.

Chapter Five

The Wedding Ceremony: Sunnah Practices

Sunnah Traditions and Etiquette of the Wedding Ceremony

As mentioned, *Nikah* is a word used for wedding ceremonies in Islam. A wedding ceremony symbolises the union of two individuals in a bond of love, respect, and responsibility, framed within the sacred teachings of the Quran and the Sunnah.

The Prophet Muhammad (PBUH) left behind valuable examples and traditions regarding wedding celebrations, underlining simplicity, joy, and spirituality. Such Sunnah practices would bring blessings to marriage and, therefore, the relationship between the two individuals and their respective families and the rest of society.

The Prophet's (PBUH) hadith states that marriage is a Sunnah act. The Prophet (PBUH) responded to one of his friends who desired to forgo marriage and devote more time to spirituality by saying,

*"...And I marry women. Whoever turns away from my
Sunnah is not of me." (Sahih Bukhari and Muslim)*

Therefore, to receive the necessary reward for marriage, it is advised
that every Muslim have this aim when getting married.

Steps Involved in the Nikkah Process

The Nikkah, or Islamic marriage contract, is essential to the marriage
process. It grants women rights that were previously denied to them in
pre-Islamic Arabia, where they had limited autonomy over their lives.
The steps involved in the Nikkah process include:

Confirming the legitimacy of the marriage: Both individuals must
meet specific criteria for the Nikkah to be valid, including being of age
and consenting freely. Islam strictly prohibits forced marriages.

Family blessings: Marriage symbolises not just the joining of two
people but also the union of families. It is important to seek family
blessings and publicly announce the Nikkah.

Representation during the ceremony: The bride needs a guardian,
typically a close male relative, while two male witnesses must be
present to validate the Nikkah. If two male witnesses are unavailable,
one male and two female witnesses may suffice.

Drafting the marriage contract: The contract outlines key details,
including the *Haq Meher* (a mandatory gift given by the groom to the
bride), and must be signed by both parties.

Consent and formalities: The officiating imam reads the contract
aloud and seeks the bride and groom's consent. This completes the
legal aspects of the Nikkah.

Islam simplifies the marriage process, emphasising that lavish celebrations are not required. The Nikkah ceremony itself is straightforward,
with only a few essential participants. However, hosting a modest re-

ception, known as Walima, is a recommended Sunnah that celebrates the occasion.

Marriage in Islam is more than a legal agreement; it is a sacred bond that forms the cornerstone of a strong and thriving society. The institution of marriage is valued not only for its personal benefits but also for its role in building cohesive communities.

Prophetic Examples of Wedding Celebrations

The weddings during the time of the Holy Prophet (PBUH) were blessed with simplicity and genuineness. One of the most well-known weddings is that of the Prophet's (PBUH) daughter, Hazrat Fatimah (RA), and Hazrat Ali (RA). This exemplifies the principle that marriage is not about ostentation but about fulfilling a Sunnah and bringing two hearts together under the mercy of Allah (SWT).

When Hazrat Fatima (RA) was about to grow up and ready to get married, many people proposed to her. The Muhammad (PBUH) received numerous proposals for her beloved daughter. Hazrat Salman Farsi (RA) and Hazrat Umm-e-Salma (RA) reported that a great number of Quraish dignitaries came to the Prophet (PBUH) to request his permission to marry her, but he rejected all of them, saying he was waiting for Allah's (SWT) word on this particular issue.

Hazrat Umm-e-Salma narrated that one day, Imam Ali (AS) went to the house of Prophet Muhammad (PBUH) to meet him. He greeted the Prophet (PBUH), who welcomed him with smiles. Then Imam Ali (AS) sat, but he was so shy that he didn't look up, nor was he able to communicate whatever he wanted to say to the Prophet (PBUH).

The Prophet (PBUH) sensed his hesitation and smiled, encouraging Imam Ali (AS) to express anything bugging him. He comforted him and told him that he was being considered to such an extent, and he had no reason to be shy about it. He knew well what Imam Ali (AS) had in his mind and what he wanted to say to him.

Encouraged by his sweet words, Imam Ali (AS) said to the Prophet (PBUH): "I have served you from my childhood and owe all that I am to your guidance. It is because of your encouragement that I feel bold enough to state my deep desire to marry one of your daughters. I have carried this desire in my heart for such a long time, not knowing if it was in tune with what you may approve of. Is it possible you would allow this to happen?" Hazrat Umm-e-Salma observed from a distance and noted that as soon as Imam Ali (AS) finished his request, the Prophet Muhammad's (PBUH) face lit up with happiness. The Prophet (PBUH) asked Imam Ali (AS) what he had to offer for the marriage. Imam Ali (AS) replied, "O Prophet (PBUH) of Allah, you know my condition. I only possess a sword, a war dress, and a camel." The Prophet Muhammad (PBUH) responded, "You will need your sword for Jihad and your camel for travel, but your war dress can serve this purpose. O Abul Hassan (AS), I bring you good news: Allah (SWT) has already decided this matter and performed your Nikah with my daughter Fatima (AS) in the heavens. Just before you arrived, an angel brought me this joyous message." (Bihar al-Anwar)

The Prophet Muhammad (PBUH) led Imam Ali (AS) to the mosque and instructed him to sell his war dress. The dress was sold for approximately 400 dirhams, which were presented to the Prophet (PBUH). He then asked Hazrat Salman Farsi (RA) and Hazrat Bilal (RA) to purchase household items for Hazrat Fatima (AS). These included mattresses, a leather mat, a pillow, a cloak, water containers, a shirt, a veil, a hand-mill, and a bed, among other things.

Upon receiving the items, the Prophet Muhammad (PBUH) visited Hazrat Fatima (AS) and informed her of the Nikah that had been performed in the heavens. He sought her consent to recite it on earth, and her shy demeanour indicated her approval. The Prophet (PBUH) then gathered the companions and recited Hamd, sharing the news of the heavenly Nikah and inviting Imam Ali (AS) to request the marriage before the witnesses formally.

Imam Ali (AS) expressed his gratitude to Allah (SWT) and requested the marriage. The Prophet Muhammad (PBUH) accepted, and the companions congratulated both Imam Ali (AS) and the Prophet (PBUH). The Nikah was concluded with a Mehr of 400 Misqaal of silver, and both the Prophet (PBUH) and Imam Ali (AS) performed Sajda-e-Shukr to Allah (SWT).

On the wedding night, Hazrat Fatima (SA) was prepared with the help of the Prophet's (PBUH) wives and adorned in a dress sent by Gabriel from Paradise. As she proceeded to Imam Ali's (AS) house, the Prophet (PBUH) led the procession, with Hazrat Jabriel (AS) and Hazrat Michael (AS) accompanied on either side by seventy thousand angels following in praise. The companions and family members joined the joyful celebration, and the Prophet (PBUH) placed Hazrat Fatima's (AS) hand in Imam Ali's (AS), completing the blessed union.

This, however, is not a denial of happiness and celebration, as Islam encourages permissible forms of celebration to mark the joyous occasion. The Prophet (PBUH) himself approved of wedding feasts (Walimah), which range from very small meals shared between a few people to large gatherings depending on the couple's circumstances.

In one instance, the Prophet's (PBUH) own Walimah was as simple as dates and water. This establishes that nothing other than material excessiveness should be centred on the happiness of the wedding.

Avoiding Extravagance (Israf) and Cultural Innovations in Weddings

The Quran forbids excess and stresses the value of balance and moderation in all facets of life, such as spending and consuming.

Allah (SWT) says, "And do not be extravagant, for verily He does not love the extravagant. And be moderate in your spending, and He (Allah) loves not the extravagant." (Quran 17:26-27)

The Holy Prophet (PBUH) said, "Allah (SWT) approves three things for you and dislikes that you do three others; he approves for you worshipping Him without partners, that you unite upon His rope, and that you do not divide among yourselves. He dislikes for you tittle-tattle, abundantly asking the people, and wasting wealth." (Sahih Bukhari & Muslim)

Therefore, the marriage ceremony in Islam is a momentous occasion, as it initiates a lifetime-sharing love relationship built upon mutual respect and duties. While it's essential to make this occasion worth remembering, there should not be extreme extravagance in its celebration nor any cultural innovation that could distract from the bond of union. Wedding customs and practices adhere closely to Islamic values, creating a spiritually meaningful celebration that provides the couple with a perfect opportunity to commit themselves to each other.

In terms of blessings (Baraka), it is best to keep the marriage ceremony and Walima (wedding party or reception) as simple as possible. Feeding individuals can cost thousands upon thousands of dollars at times; that money could be utilised to meet other essential needs for Muslims.

Additionally, it's considered a serious sin if the purpose of spending that much money is to flaunt. Here, feeding people with simplicity and honesty is the goal. Giving someone modest meals from the heart is considerably preferable to giving them fine food with less real intentions. In addition, the food tastes better.

> *The Holy Prophet (PBUH) said: "The most blessed marriage (nikah) is the one with the least expenses." (Bayhaqi, Shu'ab al-Iman)*

Balancing Cultural Customs with Islamic Values

Every culture has unique traditions surrounding weddings, often including specific customs, rituals, and celebrations. However, ensuring that these cultural practices do not contradict Islamic teachings is crucial. Balancing cultural customs with Islamic values requires mindfulness and understanding of the principles governing marriage in Islam.

In Islam, marriage is seen as a sacred and important institution and religious and cultural standards frequently serve as guidelines for choosing a life mate. Muslim marriage proposals entail a nuanced dance between past and present, and the prosperity and harmony of these unions heavily depend on cultural sensitivity.

Understanding the wide range of variety within the Muslim world is one of the most important aspects of cultural consideration in Muslim marriage proposals. Islam is practised by people of many nations, ethnic groups, and continents, resulting in diverse cultural customs. Muslims can adhere to different schools of thought, and even within the same theological denomination, cultural quirks can cause big differences. As such, one must consider suggestions for marriage with an open mind and a sincere intention to comprehend and value this difference.

Muslim marriage proposals are heavily influenced by cultural customs, which should be understood and respected to promote cultural sensitivity. For instance, some families might want a more conventional strategy in which the matchmaker includes the broader family. At the same time, others might take a more contemporary tack and involve the couple more actively in the decision-making process.

Cultural norms governing the timing and structure of marriage proposals must be carefully considered. While some cultures have complex ceremonies and rituals as standard practice, others may prefer a more straightforward, private ceremony. By honouring and adjusting these customs, the people and families participating in the proposal can guarantee a more seamless and culturally aware experience.

The manner in which Muslim marriage proposals are made has unavoidably been impacted by the changing dynamics of modern society. There is an increasing trend towards more contemporary and individualised approaches, even while cultural traditions continue to play a crucial role in the process. The essence of cultural sensitivity is finding a balance between history and modernity and honouring historical values while embracing contemporary realities.

For example, it's becoming increasingly popular to employ technology to match people. People can connect and look through possible matches on online dating platforms and matrimony websites. However, it's crucial to use cultural awareness when handling these contemporary instruments to ensure they respect Islamic beliefs and values.

While Islam encourages marriage celebrations and greater community involvement, it emphasises simplicity and avoiding waste. With these considerations, customs that promote squandering and indulgence should be balanced accordingly. In fact, the Prophet Muhammad

(PBUH) himself showed that marriage is indeed celebrated for reasons intrinsic to its spirituality rather than materialistic show-offs.

With respect to cultural customs, couples need to embrace those cultural traditions that will strengthen their marital bond and reflect shared values while avoiding practices that promote indulgence or add unnecessary stress. Family members and leaders should be present in meetings to identify those compatible with the religion of Islam. In this way, through open dialogue, the couple will respect their ancestry and yet have their wedding very much within the total principles of Islam.

Chapter Six

Rights & Responsibilities of Spouses

Mutual Rights and Obligations of Husband and Wife in Islam

I n Islam, the marital relationship is not only an element of social contract but also a sacred covenant of mutual love, respect, and understanding. The Quran and Hadith have given complete guidelines about the rights and responsibilities of both husbands and wives and put much importance on the expectations that should be met by both sides to create harmony and balance in married life. This exploring mutual rights and responsibilities forms the essence of embracing partnership and gives couples enough strength to face every hurdle that may come their way.

Islam holds that the family is a tiny social unit that comprises society. A woman and a man comprise this little unit, which is expanded through procreation. Family members share common interests, aspirations, and a deep bond. Every member of the family is only happy when the family as a whole is happy. Men and women must think about the entire family after marriage, not just themselves. A husband and wife's relationship is far more intense and almost unbreakable than that of neighbours or friends. Islam has established distinct rights and responsibilities for each spouse since it strongly supports strengthening the family unit and civilised relationships between spouses.

Roles and Responsibilities of Spouses According to Sunnah

Islam has established distinct rights and responsibilities for each spouse since it strongly supports strengthening the family unit and civilised relationships between spouses. These obligations and rights can be categorised into two primary groups: common and exclusive. These two types will be explained in the sections that follow.

The following are the common rights and obligations that apply to both husband and wife:

- **Amorousness**

Wives and husbands need to be civil to one another and practise good manners. The Quran affirms:

> *"And consort with them (your wives) in honour and equity [maruf]." (Quran 4:19)*

This verse highlights how crucial it is to treat spouses fairly, honourably, and with respect (ma'ruf), especially under trying circumstances.

The word ma'ruf, which denotes behaviour that is accepted by both reason and religion, is the antithesis of munkar, which denotes wicked behaviour. This verse is targeted at men; however, women are equally obligated to do this. Husbands and wives must treat each other with kindness, good manners, amiability, cheerfulness, compassion, helpfulness, sympathy, politeness, justice, truthfulness, support, loyalty, well-wishing, and civility.

• **Happiness and satisfaction**

While obtaining pleasure and sexual fulfilment is not the primary purpose of marriage, it is one of its main objectives and the driver of marriage. It plays a significant role in maintaining a positive working relationship between partners as well as fortifying the family unit. Therefore, one of the responsibilities of both husband and wife is to satisfy each other's needs.

When one person feels the desire to engage in sexual activity, the other should respond with readiness and not make excuses. In addition to caring about their own satisfaction, both husband and wife should take into account each other's happiness and fulfilment when making love. This is due to the fact that regular sexual gratification strengthens a couple's marriage and their family's foundation.

• **Attracting each other's attention**

Husbands and wives must respect one another's preferences for grooming, attire, beard and hairstyles, etc. Islam counsels women to wear their nicest clothes, take care of themselves, apply perfume, use cosmetics, and adorn themselves for their husbands when they are at home. Likewise, men have similar obligations towards their wives; they should maintain personal hygiene, wear nice clothes and perfume, keep their facial hair well-groomed, and look good for her.

> *A woman came to the Prophet of Allah (PBUH) and inquired, "What are the rights of a husband regarding his wife?" He replied, "Her duty is to perfume herself with the best scenting of her perfumes, and to dress in the nicest of her attires, and adorn herself with the finest of her adornments, and thus offer herself to her husband morning and night; and more than these are his rights regarding her." (Sahih Bukhari)*

Moreover, the Prophet (PBUH) stated:

> *"Each of you must prepare yourselves for your wives;*
> *just as your wives prepare themselves for you." (Al-Kafi*
> *by Shaykh al-Kulayni)*

• Bringing up and teaching children

Fathers and mothers share responsibilities for raising children, including caring for their health, developing their bodies and souls, and imparting moral and intellectual values. As a result, their participation, thoughtful consideration, and diligence are required. In this case, a mother's role is more constructive and sympathetic, but a father has a higher duty.

The following are the exclusive rights and obligations:

In Islamic tradition, men are traditionally assigned the roles of family manager, guardian, and supervisor.

> *"Men are the protectors and maintainers of women be-*
> *cause Allah (SWT) has made one of them to excel the*
> *other and because they spend (to support them) from*
> *their wealth. So righteous women are devoutly obedient,*
> *guarding in (the husband's) absence what Allah (SWT)*
> *would have them guard." (Quran 4:34)*

It is important to remember that male surveillance does not imply that the man can wield his authority to run the family selfishly, do as he pleases, and silence the viewpoints of other family members. A wise manager understands that no organisation, no matter how big or small, can be run by force or selfishness, particularly considering that the home must be a haven of safety, tranquillity, and support for children, who will grow up to shape the future of society.

The husband and wife must work together, mutually agree, and cooperatively to handle family matters; nonetheless, this small civilisation, like any other, cannot function well without a wise and powerful manager and overseer. Families without a manager typically don't have ideal circumstances. As a result, one of the wives must assume responsibility for managing and protecting the family or the husband.

These categories can be used to summarise men's supervisory responsibilities:

- Supervising family members' religious, ethical and cultural matters, assisting them in their spiritual and physical growth, and guarding the family from social and ethical decline.

- Addressing the family's needs, managing the family's income and expenses, and creating plans through consultation.

- Defending, providing for, and taking care of every family member.

- Offering monetary assistance (Nafaqah): In line with Islamic law, a man is responsible for supporting his family's daily needs

A man needs to see his wife as a gift from God and be grateful for her. He needs to respect her, treat her with kindness, overlook her errors, and avoid being stern or unyielding. Islam considers this a husband's obligation and a wife's right.

Husbands must accommodate their wives' concerns regarding beliefs, ethics, and religious practices, providing tools for learning or assisting them directly in these areas. A man ought to exercise caution over his wife's morals and behaviour, warning her against immoral actions and debaucherous conduct while encouraging her to do good activities and behave honourably. All he has to do is rescue her from the flames of Hell and extend an invitation to Heaven. This is one of the outcomes and demands of supervision, which falls under the purview of men.

> *"O you who have believed, protect yourselves and your families from a Fire whose fuel is people and stones, over which are [appointed] angels, harsh and severe; they do not disobey Allah (SWT) in what He commands them but do what they are commanded." (Quran 66:6)*

This verse emphasises the duty of Muslims to lead and defend their families by abiding by Islamic precepts and refraining from deeds that can result in transgression and punishment in the Hereafter. It highlights how crucial it is to raise virtuous and submissive children in accordance with Islamic principles.

Women's Obligations

Women bear important responsibilities towards their husbands, as emphasised in various Hadith.

> *"The jihad of a woman is to take good care of her husband." (Nahj al-Balagha)*

This encompasses not only obedience and loyalty but also fostering an environment of trust and respect. A wife supports her husband's leadership, consults him on important matters, and maintains harmony within the home. With kindness, compassion, and virtuous conduct, she nurtures a loving household. Key responsibilities include safeguarding her husband's property, upholding modesty, and seeking his permission when leaving the home (Bihar al-Anwar). Such devotion strengthens the marital bond and reflects spiritual dedication (al-Kafi).

Islam views marriage as a complete institution that supports societal stability, spiritual development, emotional fulfilment, and the continuation of the human race. When approached with sincerity and awareness, this holy tie yields immense rewards in this life as well as the next. Married couples can build a peaceful life together based on love, respect for one another, and a shared dedication to the path of justice by adhering to the teachings of the Quran and the Sunnah.

Resolving Conflicts and Maintaining Harmony in Marriage

Islam offers all people a comprehensive way of life, including peaceful marriages and effective conflict resolution. Islam is not a symbolic religion that confines itself to enforcing the requirements of devotional activities and ceremonial worship unique to a set period of time and location.

The Quran, as the primary source of law and guidance within this all-encompassing system, aims to provide a comprehensive framework that addresses judicial, societal, familial, and personal aspects of life. Allah (SWT) hopes to elevate humanity (Insan) as his vicegerents (khalifah) through this Quranic paradigm, entrusting them with the responsibility of fostering the upkeep of spiritual and temporal order and justice on earth.

When we examine the Quran, we discover that rather than just giving individuals orders to get married, most of its verses about marriage promote marital peace and conflict resolution. This demonstrates that the Quran encourages happy, long-lasting marriages, which are essential to the construction of a utopian moral society, rather than just encouraging promiscuous unions.

Given the staggering number of divorces that arise from marital discord, we must examine the Quranic teaching on this subject to understand how the scripture attempts to address these problems and lessen the potential harm that comes with high divorce rates. While

the Quran offers a recipe for marital joy and harmony, it also acknowledges that not all marriages will function flawlessly according to the
ideal model and that disputes will unavoidably arise between numerous couples for a variety of causes. Therefore, to lessen the negative
effects of such disagreement and find an acceptable settlement before
the marriage worsens, the Quran also offers comprehensive guidelines
for conflict resolution.

*Allah (SWT) says: "If you fear that a couple may break
up, appoint one arbiter from his family and one from
hers. Then, if the couple want to put things right, God
will bring about a reconciliation between them: indeed
Allah (SWT) is all knowing, all aware." (Quran 4:35)*

This is the first lesson: every marriage has difficulties, but there is
hope if you genuinely want to work at it and not give up quickly.
If you genuinely want peace, be patient with your spouse and seek
counselling or mediation; Allah (SWT) will find a way to set things
right.

Any close connection will inevitably experience conflict. Without
certain intrinsic differences, it is impossible for two people to be
emotionally close, and these disparities cause uneasiness. It is normal
for this anxiousness to be accompanied by emotions such as dread,
rage, irritation, or disappointment. When it comes to your spouse,
differences that you can tolerate with friends or even family members
can completely upend your life since you have to live with them every
day, and while you want to be very close to them, your love is not
unconditional. One thing that may either make or break a person is
marital discord. It can shatter a couple and send them into a painful
divorce, or it can strengthen a couple's bond to the point that they
experience what seems to be a taste of Jannah.

Disagreements with your spouse can also serve as a bit of a reality check, as it forces you to acknowledge that just because you want something doesn't necessarily mean it's true. We feel insecure when we disagree with our partner despite knowing intellectually that certain distinctions can be legitimate. These distinctions may be based on issues of faith, family, upbringing, politics, culture, closeness, or even something as insignificant as preferred book genres or cuisine.

Divorce can help a person grow and become a better version of themselves. Most couples don't know this, but conflict doesn't have to be the main source of tension. Individuals are not powerless victims of their emotions; they can choose how to respond to a disagreement rather than being trapped in a cycle of quarrelling and discord.

When husbands and wives in disagreement talk to a third party about their issues, they frequently come across as whiney or irate kids. She'll say that he's sluggish around the home and still dependent on his mother, while he'll grumble that she never wants to have an intimate relationship. Maybe they'll reach a compromise and begin addressing each other's needs, but both may remain vigilant, keeping score. The moment one begins to stumble, the other retreats, leading to a cycle of discontent rather than constructive resolution.

Despite providing for each other's needs, they are dissatisfied since they can't seem to figure out why or how to stop fighting over those needs. For example, even while a couple is officially fulfilling this part of their marriage from a fiqhi perspective—that is, having frequent intimate relations—they can nevertheless be deeply at odds with one another. Even when the practical aspects of marriage are taken care of, an emotional component might be ignored entirely. Despite our glances into the Prophet's (PBUH) Sunnah, many couples do not fully comprehend this everyday emotional interplay.

To resolve disagreements, we must focus more on ourselves and less on our spouses. Since we are the only ones we can alter when it comes to conflict, changing our own negative behaviour patterns is the first step in managing marital conflict. By our own attempts to eliminate the behaviour we find objectionable in our partners, we often wind up perpetuating it. Whenever we feel like blaming our spouse for something, we should stop, step back, and examine ourselves honestly. Are things truly as bad as we think they are? Are they straightforward flaws in our partner's character, or are they a response to a deeper issue that involves both of us?

If we want our relationship to improve and strengthen our bond, we must let go of resentful attempts to "punish" our partner or direct our rage against them. The goal of talking to our spouse should be to resolve a problem together as a pair, not to cast blame. Only two people who are grown enough to set aside small attempts to hurt each other can engage in constructive discussions. All we need to do is consider how we approach conversations with our spouses. This entails bringing up the topic and informing our partner of their actions' impact on us.

This calls on us to communicate with our partners in a cool, collected, and diplomatic manner. It encourages us to abandon vindictive fights, cruel words, emotional games, or passive-aggressive behaviour. Throughout this process, one thing that always needs to be kept in mind is that regardless of what our partner decides to do, we should always give our best selves to our marriage. Even if only one partner follows this path, that partner will still be a constant source of strengthening their marriage and will personally feel satisfied that they are performing half of their *deen* in a way that pleases Allah (SWT).

Another equally important component of communication is listening. Pay close attention to your partner's words and try comprehending their perspective. Refrain from talking over them or adding your own commentary. Give your partner time to complete their sentence before answering. Your lover will be more open to listening to you when you listen to them sincerely.

During arguments, we tend to concentrate on the bad things about our partner and relationship. However, practising appreciation helps settle disputes in Islamic marriages. Enjoy the good things in your marriage and relationship, and consider them blessings. This will not only help you turn your attention from the bad things in life but also make your relationship stronger.

The significance of forgiveness, endurance, and compassion in interpersonal relationships is imparted to us by the Quran. When disputes occur in your marriage, consult the Quran for advice on how to resolve the matter.

> *Allah (SWT) says: "And take provisions, but indeed, the best provision is fear of Allah (SWT). So, fear Me, O you of understanding." (Quran 2:197)*

We can set aside our egos and strive to settle problems peacefully and constructively by keeping in mind our fear of Allah (SWT).

The rights and obligations of husbands and wives occupy a prime place in an Islamic marriage. In Islam, mutual responsibilities are to be performed with love, respect, and compassion while receiving guidance from the Quran and Hadith. Effective communication by prioritising forgiveness and asking for help whenever needed can surely help spouses resolve their conflicts and keep all well-adjusted in the relationship. Lastly, upon incorporating these principles, a caring environment is achieved wherein both partners thrive toward the complete fulfilment of their roles as travelling companions.

Prophetic Examples of Kindness and Compassion Between Spouses

In marriage, mutual respect is the cornerstone of a strong bond. Islam teaches that treating your wife with respect is not only advised but necessary for creating unity. Respect entails appreciating, comprehending, and listening to one another's viewpoints. Misaligned expectations or a lack of communication are the main causes of Muslim marriage problems, but they can be resolved by fostering empathy and respect.

How can marital issues be resolved? Together, couples should practise patience, trust-building, and problem-solving. In a marriage, mutual respect ensures that each partner feels important, fortifying the marriage and keeping arguments at bay.

The Prophet (PBUH) showed his family the highest regard, virtue, and consideration. He would often ask his wives' opinions on important matters regarding the house and other things. To what extent do we ask our wives for their thoughts? The Prophet (PBUH) never raised his hands against any of his wives, indicating that he did not mistreat, say cruel things to them, or make remarks like "Ouff, why didn't you do this?" or "Why did you do that?".

A man asked the Prophet (PBUH): "What is the right of the woman over her husband?" He said: "That he should feed her as he feeds himself and clothe her as he clothes himself; he should not strike her on the face nor disfigure her, and he should not abandon her except in the house."
(Sunah Ibn Majah)

Even after the passing of his beloved wife, Hazrat Khadija, he continued to honour her memory with kindness. He treated her friends with such respect, often saying "These were Khadija's friends," giving gifts to them.

"The Prophet (PBUH) used to mention her very often. Whenever he slaughtered a sheep, he would cut it into pieces and send them to the women friends of Khadijah."
(Riyad as-Salihin)

The Prophet (PBUH) remained close to all his wives, treating them with kindness and affection. He never avoided them; instead, he paid daily visits to all of them. None of them would ever feel alone or become more envious of him for what he did. Before spending the night with the selected wife, he made it a point to see them all during the day.

Hazrat Anas (RA) said: "The Prophet (PBUH) had nine wives, and when he divided his time among them, he did not return to the first one until the ninth day. But every night, they used to gather in the house of the one whose night it was." (Sahih Muslim)

This hadith, according to Imam Nawawi, illustrates the Prophet's (PBUH) compassionate disposition and his willingness to extend kindness to everyone. (Muslim Sharh)

Hazrat Aishah (RA) said: "Every night he would go around to all of us and would come close to each wife without being intimate until he reached the one whose day it was, and he would spend the night with her." (Abu Dawood)

The hadiths mentioned above emphasise the importance of showing respect and undivided attention to our spouses. Some wives express frustration that their husbands devote more time to watching television or hanging out with friends, while many husbands feel their wives prioritise their children over their responsibilities.

Demonstrating love for your spouse is not merely a recreational activity; it should be actively expressed in their presence. The Prophet (PBUH) had to be the perfect example for us to follow as a result.

Emulating the Character of Prophet Muhammad (PBUH) in Marital Relationships

Throughout his life, the Prophet Muhammad (PBUH) showed his wives extraordinary care and compassion. In Islam, the Sunnah exemplifies behaviours that uphold compassion, kindness, and respect—especially when it comes to treating spouses.

The Prophet Muhammad (PBUH) stressed the need to provide for the material and emotional needs of spouses while also respecting their rights, creating a foundation for wholesome marriages.

Kind and Respectful Treatment

The most obvious feature of the Sunnah is dealing with wives. The Prophet (PBUH) introduced several practices that promoted conjugal love and harmonies of family life. Gentle speech was one such tenet, as Prophet Muhammad (PBUH) communicated to his wives using tender and respectful tongues, thus establishing an environment of love and understanding.

Affectionate gestures played an important role as well. Simple gestures, hugs, kisses, and verbal expressions of love were all capable of bonding two spouses emotionally.

Moreover, the Prophet (PBUH) always respected their emotions by respecting and acknowledging their feelings. This helped deepen understanding and love in a relationship. Listening impassively was another important exercise. He (PBUH) listened actively with divided attention, conveying that their words and emotions mattered, further solidifying mutual respect.

He (PBUH) always thanked his wives for their endeavours, fostering a sense of partnership rather than a master-servant dynamic. He (PBUH) showed emotional support in difficult times; he cared and understood. The Prophet (PBUH) also valued his wives' opinions, consulting them in decision-making, which reflected his respect for their viewpoints.

Avoiding harshness was paramount; He (PBUH) condemned cruelty and promoted kindness, ensuring a loving atmosphere even in disagreements. Leading by example, he (PBUH) showcased the values of compassion and respect, stating,

"The best of you are those who are best to their wives, and I am the best of you to my wives." (Tirmidhi)

Fair and just treatment

Another principle of the Sunnah is equality. The Prophet (PBUH) demonstrated equal treatment among his wives. He made sure that his time and resources were shared equally. He (PBUH) truly avoided any display of favouritism. Each wife was treated with esteem and regard in a way that squandered feelings of neglect never arose.

He (PBUH) listened to the complaints of his wives and cleared all grievances in the light of keeping harmony. He (PBUH) advocated fairness in the disputes on both sides by proposing their respective views to bring down the proper justice.

He (PBUH) also respected individuality; the Prophet understood and appreciated each one of his wives for having a different personality. He (PBUH) maintained equal provisions to fulfil their needs – be they financial or emotional – thereby giving more emphasis to equity.

Treating his wives with respect and sharing household responsibilities helped foster an environment. Upholding justice was the basis that illustrated fairness in everything and a home made up of mutual respect and peace.

One of the most vital aspects of the Sunnah is a detailed exploration of treatment towards wives as respectful and compassionate. This is an example of how to create loving and equitable relationships.

The Prophet (PBUH) demanded shared household responsibilities. He actively performed different household chores and encouraged his wives to join in family matters. Thus, such practice not only alleviated some of the burdens from his wives but also fostered mutual participation and teamwork.

Embracing this aspect of the Prophet's (PBUH) personality can help couples develop a cooperative mentality when they share responsibilities and burdens, which will ultimately result in a balanced relationship.

Chapter Seven

Building a Strong Foundation: Love and Mercy in Marriage

Islamic Perspectives on Love and Mercy Between Spouses

According to the Islamic faith, love and mercy are believed to be the cornerstones of the relationship between a husband and his wife. Along these lines, the marital bond should find itself a source of comfort, strength, and spirituality for spouses. The Quran indicates as much, positing that Allah (SWT) emphasises compassion and love in marriage and points out that these emotions are not exactly sentimental and are, rather firmly, essential in the building of a successful partnership. These perspectives guide the couples to take caring moments in creating emotional intimacy and a loving bond of respect.

Developing Emotional Intimacy and Companionship in Marriage

Emotional intimacy is crucial to a strong marriage, allowing couples to connect more deeply. This intimacy is nurtured in Islam through mutual understanding, open communication, and shared experiences. The Quran encourages spouses to support one another, as reflected in Quran which states:

"And among His signs is that He created for you from yourselves mates that you may find tranquillity in them; and He placed between you affection and mercy."
(Quran 30:21)

This verse highlights that the emotional connection between spouses is a divine blessing, intended to foster peace and security.

Meaningful conversations must occur for both partners to value each other's feelings. Through these conversations, the former also develops emotional intimacy by talking about one's thoughts, dreams, and difficulties. When one partner truly listens to the other about their worries and emotions, the open discussion is improved. This is known as active listening. The Prophet Muhammad's (PBUH) relationships with his wives, when he had to be present and attentive to their needs, amply demonstrate this.

Spending quality time together strengthens the emotional bond. Activities that both partners can participate in, such as cooking, going for walks, or sharing stories, can only strengthen the companionship inherent in a healthy marriage. The Prophet (PBUH) encouraged couples to bring joy to one another, suggesting that love thrives in an environment of happiness and laughter.

Similarly, Islam places important value on physical love for the sustenance of emotional intimacy. Hand-holding, hugging, and touching can become expressions of love and reassurance, deepening their emotional bonding. The Prophet (PBUH) was an amorous man who fully expressed love and affection in his treatment of his wives.

Cultivating a Loving and Respectful Marital Bond

Cultivating a loving and respectful marital bond requires intentional effort from both partners. In Islam, mutual respect is paramount, as emphasised in the teachings of the Quran and Hadith.

> *The Prophet Muhammad (PBUH) said, "The most perfect believers are those who are best in conduct and most kind to their families." (Tirmidhi)*

This statement underscores that kindness and respect should be foundational elements in every marital interaction.

Recognition of each other's individuality and the unique skills every spouse brings into the union is one of the building blocks of mutual respect. Valued and appreciated strengths and viewpoints from both spouses complement and enrich the overall marriage dynamic. Enjoying each other's successes and celebrating each other through hard times will build trust and loyalty in the marriage.

Further, forgiveness is a must in marriage. Conflicts and misunderstandings will inevitably come to the forefront, but how couples address and resolve them determines the strength of their bond. Islam teaches the people forgiveness, as pointed out to the Prophet (PBUH) when he urged his followers to overlook faults and try to reconcile. It lays down a culture of understanding and healing, where couples can let go of past grievances and grow together.

Another essential component of a good marriage is communication. Open and courteous communication of needs, feelings, and concerns should be a goal for couples. The Prophet Muhammad (PBUH) taught that couples should communicate openly and gently about their problems, emphasising the value of clarity in communication. This method not only settles disputes but also builds trust and a sense of security in the partnership.

It further strengthens the spiritual relationship in the marriage. Couples pray together, read the Quran, and engage in charitable activities, strengthening the purpose and feelings toward one's religion. It also strengthens the emotional relationship as couples encourage each other using their faith and development.

The Islamic perspective on love and compassion between spouses can serve as a basis for developing emotional intimacy as well as respectful and loving marital bonds. Acceptance of the beliefs about compassion, mutual respect, and open communication at home nurture that kind of relationship.

The life of the Prophet is an example of how kindness and love can form a strong and happy marriage for those who are married, offering guidance for those seeking to develop a fruitful partnership grounded in the beauty of Islamic teachings. When spouses work on developing emotional attachment and a spirit of love and mercy in relationships, their marriage thrives with solidity and harmony and, hence, easily get along with the pressure or difficulty that life may throw at them.

The Concept of Rahmah (Mercy) in Marital Relationships

In Islam, the concept of *Rahmah*, or mercy, plays a pivotal role in marital relationships, embodying compassion, forgiveness, and a deep sense of empathy that should permeate every aspect of a couple's life together. The essence of Rahmah not only contributes to individual well-being but also fortifies the marital bond, creating an environment conducive to love, understanding, and harmony. This profound principle is exemplified in the Quran and the teachings of Prophet Muhammad (PBUH), guiding couples toward a nurturing relationship rooted in mercy.

Practising Forgiveness and Empathy in Marriage

Forgiveness is a cornerstone of any successful marriage, and in Islam, it is regarded as an essential expression of Rahmah. Recognising that both partners are human and prone to mistakes fosters an environment where forgiveness is readily offered.

The truth is that everyone is in a state of ongoing growth, and nobody is flawless. What is the process by which they develop? Their life experiences and missteps—many involving other people—help them grow. Since humans are fallible beings who occasionally make mistakes and commit sins, we cannot hold others to high standards.

Rather, we ought to provide space for pardoning, just as the revered Prophet (PBUH) did. We should make every effort to foster a culture of forgiveness in Islam since Allah (SWT), the Most Merciful and Forgiving, also pardons the transgressions of His Servants!

Forgiveness is a fundamental quality in the magnificent persona of the Prophet Muhammad (PBUH). Numerous prophetic stories highlight his remarkable capacity for forgiveness and how it ultimately leads to a fulfilling spiritual experience. He did not take offence at non-Muslims' disdain for him. Rather, he was always nice and patient with them, ultimately transforming those he encountered into good Muslims, SubhanAllah.

Particularly during his terrible ordeal in Taif, he lost both his wife and his cherished uncle. There, the people of the tribe stoned him, and the city officials ridiculed him impolitely. He had confidence in Allah (SWT) and only desired to please Him, never making dua to get revenge on the tribesmen who had hurt him. Forgiveness is a quality of the brave and the patient, so we should work to become forgiving Muslims—even if it can be really challenging at times.

Reconciliation and forgiveness can be a reaction to perceived injustice. There are two types of dispute resolution processes: external and internal. One advantage of reconciliation is that it usually results in a smaller injustice gap for the victim.

The offender typically exhibits weak behaviours, like saying sorry, which can benefit the victim by giving the circumstance a stronger sense of justice. This will not only encourage reconciliation but also improve the chance of forgiveness. The act of forgiving is what defines the forgiver. Reconciliation within oneself is made possible by forgiveness, which in turn permits forgiveness of others and may result in reconciliation.

Our psychological and physical health can be severely impacted by conflict and social injury, and some people contend that our ability to cope with and move past these trying and painful situations plays a major role in determining our level of pleasure. Depending on the relationship, forgiveness can appear differently when forgiving a stranger than a loved one.

The capacity for both forgiving and asking for forgiveness is a major aspect of marital pleasure. It is frequently cited as one of the most crucial elements influencing a relationship's lifespan. Empathy, attributions, and relationship quality have all been related to forgiveness in marriages.

The Quran emphasises the importance of forgiving others, stating:

> *"Let not those of virtue among you and wealth swear not to give to their near relatives and the needy and those who have emigrated for the cause of Allah (SWT). And let them pardon and overlook. Would you not like that Allah (SWT) should forgive you? And Allah (SWT) is Forgiving and Merciful." (Quran 24:22)*

This verse underscores the value of forgiveness as a path to divine mercy, encouraging spouses to extend this same grace to one another.

The fact that there are hardships and misfortunes in the world of Dunya is yet another explanation for why everyone should be prepared to forgive. Accepting the tests is equivalent to accepting Allah's (SWT) Divine Decree, acknowledging that the traumatic event you experienced was intended. For some people, this may be a gradual process, while for others, it may take a lifetime. Allah (SWT) will also use other people to test us.

> *"...And We have made some of you as a trial for others –*
> *will you have patience? And ever is your Lord, Seeing."*
> *(Quran 25:20)*

Practising empathy involves understanding and sharing the feelings of one's spouse, creating a strong emotional connection. When couples strive to comprehend each other's experiences and emotions, they can respond with compassion, validating their feelings.

Our beloved Prophet (PBUH) exhibited emotional empathy for his wives in numerous ways. He was well renowned for showing his wives how much he loved them without holding back, and he provided us with several examples of how to be kind to our partners.

> *Hazrat Aisha (RA), his wife (PBUH), told the story: "It*
> *was the day of Id, and the Ethiopian people were playing*
> *with shields and spears; so either I requested the Prophet*
> *(PBUH) or he asked me whether I would like to see the*
> *display. I replied in the affirmative. Then the Prophet*
> *(PBUH) made me stand behind him, and my cheek was*
> *touching his cheek, and he was saying, "Carry on! O*
> *Bani Arfida," till I got tired. The Prophet (PBUH) asked*
> *me, "Are you satisfied (Is that sufficient for you)?" I*
> *replied in the affirmative, and he told me to leave."*
> *(Sahih Bukhari)*

According to this hadith, our dear Prophet (PBUH) considered his wife's emotional desire for happiness and satisfaction when it came to permissible amusement.

> *Narrated by Hazrat Anas (RA): "It reached Safiyyah that Hafsah called her: 'The daughter of a Jew,' so she (Safiyyah) wept. Then the Prophet (PBUH) entered upon her while she was crying, and he said: 'What makes you cry?' She said: 'Hafsah said to me that I am the daughter of a Jew.' So the Prophet (PBUH) said: 'And you are the daughter of a Prophet (PBUH), and your uncle is a Prophet (PBUH), and you are married to a Prophet (PBUH), so what is she boasting to you about?' Then he said: 'Fear Allah (SWT), O Hafsah.'" (Tirmidhi)*

Without causing harm to anyone, our beloved Prophet (PBUH) would console his wives with humour and kind words because he cared about their sentiments.

The Prophet Muhammad (PBUH) exemplified deep empathy for the struggles and challenges faced by his wives. By adopting a similar approach, couples can cultivate a deeper understanding of each other, leading to a more supportive and nurturing environment.

In moments of conflict or misunderstanding, practising forgiveness and empathy becomes especially crucial. It is essential to approach disagreements with a mindset focused on resolution rather than blame.

By acknowledging each other's perspectives and emotions, spouses can de-escalate tensions and work toward reconciliation. The ability to forgive allows couples to move past grievances, reinforcing the marital bond and fostering resilience against future challenges.

Chapter Eight

Intimacy and Sexual Ethics in Islam

Understanding the Islamic Perspective on Intimacy and Sexual Relations

E very Muslim is obligated to abide by Islamic law in all aspects of his life, from prayer and fasting to marriage. One must be aware of the laws and customs surrounding marriage to completely adhere to Islam. These laws are divinely inspired and designed to respect, rather than suppress, natural human emotions.

Following these teachings not only keeps a person committed to their faith but also shields them from the deluge of sex literature that depicts this natural impulse as something that must be allowed to run amok.

While Western views on sexual freedom often encourage permissiveness, Islam prohibits certain acts considered immoral, not to violate someone's right to freedom, but to safeguard both spiritual development and physical health. Furthermore, in societies where complete sexual freedom is the norm, we witness the degeneration of society.

In Islam, intimacy and sexual relations within marriage are viewed as natural and essential aspects of the marital bond. They are not merely physical acts but are also deeply spiritual, reflecting the love, compassion, and mutual respect that should characterise a healthy marriage. The teachings of the Quran and the Sunnah guide how couples can navigate intimacy in a way that aligns with Islamic values, ensuring that their physical relationship is both fulfilling and respectful.

Importance of Sex in Marriage

Islam does not limit marriage to a platonic union of husband and wife or to the purpose of bearing children. Nikah, the Islamic term for marriage, literally translates to "sexual relations". So why has Islam established so many laws and guidelines pertaining to sexual matters?

This was due to Islam's complete comprehension that sexual impulses cannot and should not be suppressed. They can only be controlled for the benefit of people's welfare in this life as well as their prosperity in the next.

> *"They ask you concerning menstruation. Say: It is a harmful thing, so keep away from women during menstruation and do not approach them until they are purified. And when they have purified themselves, then approach them in the manner Allah has commanded you. Truly, Allah loves those who turn to Him in repentance and loves those who purify themselves." (Quran 2:222)*

This verse guides the relations between husband and wife, specifically concerning the menstruation period and the command to refrain from intimate relations during that time, resuming only after the wife has purified herself.

The innate need for sex is powerful and important. To meet their sexual demands in a safe and comfortable setting, everyone ought to have a partner. Everyone ought to experience sexual fulfilment in the right and appropriate way. Individuals who choose not to get married frequently experience psychological and/or physical health issues. Teenage abstinence from marriage is a direct cause of these diseases and several social issues. When two believers get married and start a family, their sexual interactions will help them grow in their love and kindness for one another. There won't be any threats of sexual perversion, harmful addictions, or illegal acts for this kind of couple.

There are three reasons why discussing sexual morality is important. The first is that it is relevant to all Muslims. First, there is a consensus among Muslims that everyone must adhere to the Shariah or Islamic regulations; these laws extend beyond the confines of prayer, fasting, worship, and other ceremonial practices. The Shariah provides particular guidelines regarding sex.

Therefore, just as Muslims must learn how to complete the daily prayers, so too must they understand Islam's position on sexual morality to fully embrace the religion. Second, it cannot be overstated how important it is for Muslims exposed to the New Sexual Ethics of the West to understand Islamic sexual morality. Thirdly, parents today need to understand what is appropriate and inappropriate when it comes to sex education for their children because youngsters in the West receive an excessive amount of it beyond the comprehension of earlier generations. The only parent who can handle this issue effectively and responsibly is a Muslim who is well-informed.

Because Islamic Shariah is all-encompassing, Islamic sexual morality differs fundamentally from other moralities. Islam acknowledges that people have sexual wants and desires and teaches that these impulses should be embraced rather than suppressed. According to Islam, the biological components of our bodies have a purpose; they are not made for nothing. Nowhere in Islamic scriptures teaches that having intercourse is inherently bad or sinful; rather, all that the Prophet Muhammad (PBUH), the Ahlu'l-bayt, and the Quran have taught is the reverse.

What the genuine sunnah, the Quran, and myself stressing authenticity have to say regarding marriage and sex will now be covered under the following headings: Islam has always aggressively advocated marriage as a good deed rather than as the lesser of two evils. It also strongly opposes celibacy and monasticism and holds that marriage does not impede spiritual travel but rather aids it.

The Prophet (PBUH) and the Ahlu'l Bayt Imams also urged his adherents to get married and indulge in their sexual cravings in moderation. The Islamic perspective on the wonderful things in this world is not pessimistic; rather, it teaches that we should recognise them as God-given gifts. Thus, Islam is completely against celibacy and monasticism.

'Uthman bin Maz'un was one of the Prophet's (PBUH) close companions. His spouse once protested to the Prophet (PBUH), saying, "O the Messenger of God! 'Uthman fasts during the day and stands for prayers during the night." Put differently, she intended to convey that her spouse was refraining from having sex both during the day and at night.

This infuriated the Prophet (PBUH) so greatly that he didn't even wait to put on his slippers. Carrying the slippers, he emerged and proceeded to 'Uthman's residence. He was caught praying by the Prophet (PBUH). Upon completing his prayers, 'Uthman faced the Prophet (PBUH), who exclaimed, "O 'Uthman! Allah (SWT) provided me with a straightforward and uncomplicated message, not a monastic one [shari'ah]. I pray, fast, and engage in close physical contact with my spouse. Therefore, if someone enjoys my customs, he should adhere to them; one of my traditions is marriage." The word "marriage" in this hadith refers primarily to sexual interactions because 'Uthman was already married.

> The Prophet (PBUH) said, "Two rak'ats (cycles) prayed
> by a married person are better than the night vigil and
> the fast of a single person." (Sahih Bukhari)

The Prophet (PBUH) was approached by a woman who claimed she had tried everything in vain to get her husband to notice her; he refused to break out of his meditation to give her any attention. The Prophet (PBUH) instructed her to tell her husband about the benefits of having sex, which he explained as follows.

"When a man approaches his wife, he is guarded by two angels and [at that moment in Allah's view] he is like a warrior fighting for the cause of Allah. When he has intercourse with her, his sins fall like the leaves of the tree [in fall season]. When he performs the major ablution, he is cleansed from sins." (Ihya Ulum al-Din)

Guidelines for Maintaining Purity and Chastity within Marriage

Islam emphasises the importance of purity and chastity, integral to a fulfilling marital relationship. This purity is not only physical but also moral and spiritual. Couples are encouraged to uphold high ethical standards and engage in their relationship with a sense of responsibility.

"And they who are to their trusts and their covenant due. And they who carefully maintain their prayer: They will be in gardens, honoured." (Quran 23:5-7)

This verse underscores the significance of trust and responsibility within the marital relationship.

To maintain a holy marriage, both husbands and wives need to feel emotionally and spiritually connected. Such a connection can create an atmosphere wherein intimacy will flourish without desecration of the marriage. Periodic joint acts of worship, like daily prayers and recitation of the Quran, can strengthen such a bond. Beyond that, couples should openly express their needs and desires toward each other. The parties involved will feel appraised and respected for their work.

Chastity in marriage also refers to being cautious of the external elements that can damage the relationship. Couples must avoid situations that will tempt them or make them have sexual intercourse outside the official channel. Limiting themselves from some friends and relatives may help preserve the matrimony's holy nature. Fidelity and loyalty are one of the cruxes of the Islamic doctrine; each marriage partner should pledge themselves to one another.

Mutual Rights and Etiquette in Physical Intimacy

In Islam, physical intimacy is not merely a physical act but a profound expression of love and affection. The Quran acknowledges the importance of this aspect of marriage, describing spouses as "garments" for one another:

> *"They are clothing for you, and you are clothing for them." (Quran 2:187)*

This metaphor emphasises the deep connection and intimacy that spouses share, highlighting the importance of mutual rights and responsibilities.

Both spouses have the right to fulfil their longings and satisfy their marital pleasures; open communication is essential. Prophet Muhammad (PBUH) did this by emphasising open communication of intimacy with consent, ensuring that both spouses understand and consent to it. The applicability of emphasis on consent is that both should feel comfortable and esteemed in sexual life.

Intimate relationship etiquette is just as important as Islamic doctrine. How the Prophet (PBUH) described intimacy is how it should be handled. He made the case that the custom should be kind, considerate, and compassionate. He advised them to love one another more than to use the act and to keep each other's feelings in mind throughout the process. Certain behaviours, such as expressing love and thanks, could enhance the enjoyment of the encounter for both people.

However, Islam emphasises hygienic practices and cleanliness during sexual activity. Maintaining hygiene is not just a matter of health but also serves as a way for spouses to show respect and consideration for each other. Islamic teachings also outline specific guidelines regarding the timings for coital intercourse, prohibiting intimacy during a woman's menstrual cycle and postpartum period. During these times, women are encouraged to refrain from having coital interactions with their husbands.

The fundamental understanding of intimacy and sexual intercourse in the context of marriage is mutual respect, emotional binding, and observance of morality and spirituality. Purification and chastity are also relevant because they reflect a commitment to self and faith. A couple can have an enjoyable and harmonious marital relationship if they maintain open communication and learn from mutual rights and etiquette in sexual intercourse. Ultimately, these teachings may culminate in a love and compassion bonding that mixes spiritual and healthy fulfilment in an Islamic marriage.

Addressing Common Questions and Concerns Related to Marital Intimacy

Marital intimacy in Islam is a significant aspect of the relationship between husband and wife. However, it is often accompanied by numerous questions and concerns. Addressing these inquiries ensures couples understand their rights and responsibilities while cultivating a fulfilling and ethical marital bond. Central to this understanding are the principles of consent, mutual satisfaction, and the prophetic teachings on intimacy and sexual ethics.

Importance of Consent and Mutual Satisfaction in Islamic Marriage

Building a foundation for any intimate relationship, mutual respect, love, and understanding are viewed as requirements in Islam. One of the essentials in marital intimacy is the sanctity of consent. Partners should be comfortable and willing to engage in sexual relations; otherwise, it leads to the mockery of intercourse, becoming a means for pleasure and bonding instead of obligation or coercion. In fact, the Quran essentially teaches that mutual rights exist for spouses, referring to the satisfaction and emotional fulfilment between spouses.

The Prophet Muhammad (PBUH) is also an example of this, even in marital relations, because he ensured all parties involved had their consent; thus, he maintained mutual satisfaction for his wives. Indeed, this laid a healthy environment where both partners could easily clarify their desires and boundaries. Therefore, trust among couples is established by such discussions over one's needs and expectations, which enhances the emotional relationship.

Mutual satisfaction does not inherently involve some form of physical gratification; it also involves emotional and spiritual fulfilment. When a relationship prioritises the respective partner's needs and wants, the bond becomes stronger by being in harmony. According to that definition, intimacy must be two-way, emphasising each other's pleasure and satisfaction, making it a more enjoyable experience for both.

Prophetic Teachings on Marital Intimacy and Sexual Ethics

Teachings of the Prophet Muhammad (PBUH) provide a guiding framework for marital intimacy and sexual ethics in Islam. His life provides insights on how couples can maintain intimacy respectfully and compassionately. The Prophet (PBUH) highlighted that cohabitation should be done with love and tenderness; besides physical attraction, emotional relationship matters.

His teachings as Prophet (PBUH) taught that intimacy should be grounded in love and respect. He encouraged spouses to treat each other well, teaching that the best of you are those who are best to their families, and he declared himself to be the best among them. This principle is extended into marital intimacy, wherein everything has to be laced with love and care.

The Prophet (PBUH) also addressed the practical instructions on sexual ethics. His message was that intercourse should be approached with a sense of balance and respect for modesty, highlighting the importance of maintaining an intimate yet humble relationship between spouses. His message further emphasised that privacy within the marriage is essential; discussing their intimate life is not discussed outside the marriage fosters a sense of mutual trust and security.

He taught hygiene and cleanliness as a basic attitude in marital relations. He instructed his followers to maintain personal hygiene and cleanliness, for this would not only show respect for each other but also contribute to the health of both partners. There is a ritual of purification, such as ghusl, or full-body purification for sexual actions, which further emphasises the importance of cleanliness in marital intimacy.

One of the essential elements is to take care of common questions that develop anxiety around marital intimacy between spouses in Islam. Consent and mutual satisfaction are considered the main principles of intimacy, where each partner feels valued and respected. The prophetic teachings on marital intimacy and sexual ethics have framed this aspect of the relationship with love, compassion, and understanding.

This teaching instilled in them respect between a man and a woman toward each other. It encourages complete open communication. By embracing these teachings and open communication, couples can build a strong and intimate bond; the true essence of Islamic marriage scholars is mutually respectful, emotionally connected, and spiritually fulfilling.

Chapter Nine

Financial Management and Household Responsibilities

Financial Rights and Responsibilities of Spouses in Islam

I n Islamic marriage, financial rights and responsibilities are clearly defined to ensure that both partners are treated fairly and equitably. The principles governing financial matters in marriage are grounded in the Quran and the Sunnah, emphasising the importance of mutual support, collaboration, and accountability. By understanding these financial rights and responsibilities, couples can foster a harmonious household where both partners feel secure and respected.

Islamic Principles of Wealth Distribution and Financial Support within Marriage

Islamic teachings on financial matters prioritise the well-being and dignity of both spouses. According to the Quran, husbands are primarily responsible for providing for their families, as stated:

> *"Men are the protectors and maintainers of women be-*
> *cause of what Allah (SWT) has given one over the oth-*
> *er and because of what they spend from their wealth."*
> *(Quran 4:34)*

This verse emphasises the husband's duty to provide for the needs of his wife and family, which includes shelter, food, clothing, and other necessities.

However, this responsibility is not one-sided. While the man is tasked with providing for the home, the woman also has the right to financial support. In Islam, the mahr or dowry serves to further secure the right of the woman to economic provisions. Mahr is a provision of money that is required to be given to the bride at or before the consummation of the marriage. In this way, it is a testament to respect and commitment to the other person. Whatever she may earn through her work or investments is also hers, and the husband does not have any claims to it unless she voluntarily gives him some.

However, in Islam, a harmonious marriage expects the couple to make joint financial decisions, considering each other's desires and needs. It encourages openness in their communications regarding finances, goals, and life's burdens so they can live harmoniously. For that reason, it establishes partnership and respect for one another.

Budgeting and Financial Planning for a Harmonious Household

Budgeting and financial planning play crucial roles in keeping the house harmonious. Islamic teachings advocate responsible financial management, which means that both partners should work together to create a budget that fulfils all their needs, goals, and values.

Any good budget will, of course, enumerate sources of income and propose necessary household expenses such as shelter, food, utilities, education, health bills, and savings. Couples should prioritise these expenses first so that at least all the primary needs of a couple are met. Then, funds are allocated for discretionary spending. Islam has prescribed *takaful* or mutual assistance that enables spouses to work together whenever they need and share resources, further driving home this point.

Long-term financial planning should go beyond just budgeting. It may involve saving for the future to meet a child's education, retirement, or emergency funds. The Prophet Muhammad (PBUH) urged prudent financial planning and foresight by explaining that it is wise to anticipate future needs and prepare for them. Such an approach will help reduce the stress on finances, give a feeling of security, and support both partners.

Moreover, Islamic teachings emphasise avoiding extravagance and wastefulness in financial matters. The Quran warns against israf (extravagance) as:

> *"Eat and drink, but be not excessive. Indeed, He likes not those who commit excess." (Quran 7:31)*

By practising moderation in spending and being mindful of financial resources, couples can cultivate a more harmonious and sustainable household.

The fact that Islam has applied the principle of mutuality in the distribution of a couple's wealth ensures respect between partners, giving both persons concerned a sense of security and value.

Effective budgeting and financial planning are required to maintain this balance in a couple's financial landscape. To better understand the good foundations of the household, the couple will be endowed with cooperation, mutual understanding, and goals based on these Islamic teachings. Ultimately, a sound financial partnership only fosters a more whole and lucrative marriage.

Division of Household Chores and Responsibilities

In Islamic marriage, the division of household chores and responsibilities is essential for fostering harmony and collaboration between spouses. A successful partnership is built on shared responsibilities, where both partners contribute to the well-being of the family. By drawing upon prophetic examples and Islamic teachings, couples can achieve a balanced and equitable division of household tasks that reflects mutual respect and cooperation.

Prophetic Examples of Shared Responsibilities Between Spouses

The life of the Prophet Muhammad (PBUH) offers invaluable insights into the importance of shared responsibilities within marriage. He exemplified a balanced approach to household duties, actively participating in domestic tasks alongside his wives. For instance, it is narrated in the hadith that the Prophet (PBUH) would help with chores, such as cleaning, cooking, and caring for children. This practice not only demonstrated his commitment to family life but also emphasised the significance of partnership in managing household affairs.

One specific instance that highlights the Prophet's (PBUH) involvement is when he assisted with the preparation of meals and performed other tasks in the home. His example encourages couples to communicate openly about their roles and responsibilities, ensuring that both partners feel valued and included in household management. The Prophet's (PBUH) actions reflect the Islamic principle that both husband and wife are responsible for creating a nurturing and harmonious environment for their family.

Moreover, the Prophet's (PBUH) interactions with his wives showed a spirit of cooperation and mutual support. He recognised their individual strengths and encouraged them to contribute in ways that suited their abilities and circumstances. This approach not only fostered a sense of teamwork but also promoted understanding and respect.

Achieving Balance and Equity in Managing Household Affairs

Achieving balance and equity in household responsibilities requires open communication, mutual respect, and flexibility. Couples should discuss their individual strengths, preferences, and workloads to ensure that tasks are divided in a way that feels fair and manageable for both. This collaborative approach promotes a sense of teamwork, where both feel they have an equal stake in the household's well-being.

To establish a fair division of chores, couples can start by listing household tasks and identifying who best suits each role. For example, if one partner enjoys cooking while the other prefers cleaning, it is logical for them to take on those respective duties. However, it is crucial to avoid rigid roles; instead, couples should be open to switching tasks when necessary or during busy periods.

Flexibility and understanding are vital when navigating household responsibilities. Life circumstances, such as work schedules or personal commitments, may necessitate adjustments in the division of chores. Couples should be willing to communicate openly about their changing needs and adapt their responsibilities accordingly. This willingness to accommodate each other's circumstances fosters a supportive environment where both partners feel respected and valued.

Additionally, it is essential to recognise that household responsibilities extend beyond physical chores. Emotional support, decision-making, and planning for the future are equally important aspects of managing a household. Couples should strive for a holistic partnership where both partners are actively involved in all dimensions of family life.

The division of household chores and responsibilities in an Islamic marriage reflects mutual respect, cooperation, and commitment to family life. By following the prophetic examples of shared responsibilities, couples can create a nurturing environment where both partners feel valued and supported.

Achieving balance and equity in household affairs requires open communication, flexibility, and a willingness to adapt to changing circumstances. Ultimately, a collaborative approach to household responsibilities strengthens the marital bond, fostering a harmonious and fulfilling life together.

Chapter Ten

Parenting and Family Life in Islam

Islamic Perspectives on Parenting and Raising Children

A good upbringing is the best gift that parents can give their children. But with so many parenting philosophies to choose from, it's easy to feel overwhelmed or unsure about how to raise honourable and productive children! These simple guidelines offer essential steps for effective parenting and fostering responsible, capable young adults.

For Muslims, children are both a duty and a blessing—an *amanah*. Our responsibility is to nurture them into hardworking, fruitful, and, above all, God-fearing people who will benefit the Ummah.

> *The Prophet Muhammad (PBUH) said, "When a man dies, his action discontinues from him except three things, namely, perpetual sadaqah (charity), or the knowledge by which benefit is acquired, or a pious child who prays for him." (Sunan Abi Dawud)*

Parenting in Islam is a profound responsibility that encompasses the nurturing of children in both physical and spiritual dimensions. Parents need to instil Islamic values and character in their children, guiding them toward becoming righteous and responsible individuals. Through the Quran and Sunnah teachings, parents can create a family environment that fosters spiritual growth, ethical behaviour, and a deep connection to their faith.

Therefore, our goal and objective should be to raise our kids so that they would benefit both us and themselves in the Hereafter. Here are a few guidelines that we must constantly keep in mind as we go about our everyday responsibilities of raising our kids to accomplish this goal:

Parents serve as mentors and exemplars: While they are young, children are still learning what is right and wrong. For children to carry on with good and pure deeds, it is the parent's duty to teach them how to accomplish this, how to select their surroundings, and what kind of people to surround themselves with.

> *Allah's Messenger (PBUH) said, "Everyone of you is a guardian and is responsible for his charges. The ruler who has authority over people is a guardian and is responsible for them; a man is a guardian of his family and is responsible for them; a woman is a guardian of her husband's house and children and is responsible for them; a slave is a guardian of his master's property and is responsible for it; so all of you are guardians and are responsible for your charges." (Sahih Bukhari)*

Children, still learning about the world, often don't know the right path to take. Above all, they need to be nurtured. Parents are responsible for caring, leading, and providing guidance. If left unguided, a child may be influenced in various directions by the people he encounters.

However, when parents take seriously their duty to raise him upon the principles of Al-Fitr – the natural disposition towards goodness – and to follow Allah (SWT) and His Messenger (PBUH), he is more likely to remain on a path that is righteous and pure.

Kids are pure from birth. A person's behaviour can be viewed in two ways: either his actions are determined by his internal qualities or tied to his circumstances. This is social psychology's theory of attribution.

However, The Holy Prophet (PBUH) said: "No child is born except on Al-Fitra (Islam or primordial human nature), and then his parents make him Jewish, Christian or Magian, as an animal produces a perfect young animal: do you see any part of its body amputated?"
(Sahih Muslim)

According to this hadith, children are born pure and blameless, with a natural tendency for virtue and a belief in the one Allah (SWT). This means there is no chance that a child's intrinsic qualities will lead him to misbehave. Therefore, holding a child responsible for whatever they do wrong is impossible, especially before they are ten.

A child's main objective is to mimic or apply what he has observed, heard, felt, and learnt from his surroundings.

The virtues of mercy and kindness are fundamental to parenting: Having compassion for the people under your direction is a hallmark of a strong leader. This attribute belonged to the Prophet Muhammad (PBUH), who showed compassion and mercy to everyone, even his opponents, whom he did not lead.

Our Prophet (PBUH) was kinder to children whom he would let climb over him while in prostration.

It was narrated from 'Abdullah bin Shaddad (RA) that his father said: "The Messenger of Allah (PBUH) came out to us for one of the nighttime prayers, and he was carrying Hasan (RA) or Husain (RA). The Messenger of Allah (PBUH) came forward and put him down, then he said the Takbir and started to pray. He prostrated during his prayer and made the prostration lengthy." My father said: "I raised my head and saw the child on the back of the Messenger of Allah (PBUH) while he was prostrating, so I went back to my prostration. When the Messenger of Allah (PBUH) finished praying, the people said: "O Messenger of Allah (PBUH), you prostrated during the prayer for so long that we thought that something had happened or that you were receiving a revelation.' He said: 'No such thing happened. But my son was riding on my back, and I did not want to disturb him until he had had enough." (Sunah an-Nasa'i)

The Prophet Muhammad (PBUH) did not forbid children from playing, recognising it as a part of a child's natural behaviour. We, too, have to realise that a child's play and "kidding around" are essential to their healthy development, supporting social, emotional, mental, and physical growth. These principles are the fundamental tenets of Islamic childrearing. Taking action on them eases the burden of parenthood a little.

Roles of Parents in Nurturing Islamic Values and Character in Children

The Messenger of Allah (PBUH) and his family have said, "Acquaint your children with religious teachings (of Islam) before the disbelievers get to them." (Sahih Muslim)

After you have studied and reviewed your religion and worship style, including its rites and customs, discuss with your partner what is most important to you. Though many of the theoretical ideas of your faith may be beyond the grasp of your younger children, keep in mind that they will learn about faith via your words, deeds, and interactions with your spouse.

The "first" madressa lesson for our children should be when they are born, and the proud parents recite the Adhan and Iqamah in their right and left ears, respectively. We must foster Islamic teachings in our children as early as possible, even before the mother becomes pregnant. Parents must have sufficient knowledge to instruct their children and set them on the path of study and a desire to learn more about Islam, even though it is acknowledged that they may not be spiritual leaders of the faith.

> *When the Prophet (PBUH) and his family turned to face some small children, they uttered the following: "Woe be upon the children of the latter days from that which their fathers will do (to them)." It was said, 'O Messenger of Allah! From their fathers, who are polytheists? He replied, 'No! From their fathers, who are believers, however, they do not teach them anything from the (religious) obligations and whatever they teach their children from the (transient) world, they only teach them that amount which will allow them to "get by" with ease. Indeed, I am not from them, nor are they from me." (Sahih Bukhari)*

The Prophet (PBUH) of Mercy makes a strong and significant declaration for many reasons, as it addresses both the spiritual lessons and this fleeting world. In this brief saying, he demonstrates to us that the Prophet (PBUH) was not only looking at fathers who did not even teach their children about the world in which we live but also that it is not sufficient for the father (and mother) to focus solely on "spiritual teachings"—though these are very important. All parents must ensure they impart the faith and its comprehensive nature to the next generation!

Where can our children go to get such pearls of knowledge when there are so many life skills not provided for in the public school system and so many more things that we need to teach them but are not done in a Madressa system? Are we really expecting kids to search Google for every answer?

They'll probably turn to their friend, some of whom might not have the right morals and may teach them things that aren't always what we want them to learn. This could lead to the spiritual devastation of their souls. As a result, we must make every effort to teach our children about the environment in which we live, how to navigate it, and how to avoid the system's purposefully created traps and limitations.

We can try our best to provide our children with the necessary tools to enter the spiritual and spatial worlds with both feet firmly planted in the footsteps of the Quran and the Prophetic traditions, as explained by the noble Ahlul Bayt (PBUH). Granted, things change from generation to generation, and what may be true today may not be the same for our children.

Building a Family Environment Based on Quranic Teachings

Creating a loving family environment is essential in bringing up children according to the principles of Islam. Parents must strive for homes that are certainly according to the teachings of the Quran, where love, respect, and compassion are paramount. This provides a platform for children to develop their character and/or faith.

One of the key conditions in developing such a setting is mutual respect and understanding among family members. Parents should model respectful communication to their children and show them how to go about constructive dialogue and resolve conflicts amicably. A third example comes from the significance of benevolence and respect within family relationships in the words of the Prophet Muhammad (PBUH): "He who does not show mercy to our young and does not respect our elders is not one of us." This value teaches that there ought to be compassion and respect in a family.

Another thing is to be grateful and appreciate Allah's favours (SWT), which is important to a healthy family atmosphere. Parents can constantly tell their children to feel grateful for the blessings received to promote the right attitude of thankfulness and humility. This can be done by remembering how gratitude is important in Islam.

Parents should also promote a culture of learning within the family. Encouraging children to seek knowledge and engage in educational pursuits aligns with the Islamic principle of valuing education.

> *The Prophet Muhammad (PBUH) said, "Seeking knowledge is an obligation upon every Muslim." (Sunan Ibn Majah)*

By supporting their children's education and instilling a love for learning, parents contribute to their overall development and empowerment.

The Islamic view considers parenting a vital source of heavy responsibility for parents to acquire their children's intellectual and moral development. Thus, parents themselves, to help their children become ideal Muslims, will need to promote a family environment fitting for implementing Quranic teachings.

Open communication, respect for each other, and commitment to developing thankfulness and love for learning must form that basis. Ultimately, a good upbringing is founded on Islamic principles, generally equipping children to grow up as well-rounded persons with knowledge about their religion and enthusiasm for attaining its teachings.

Maintaining Ties with Extended Family and Relatives

Islam values the family highly and views it as the foundation of society. Families are essential for raising morally upright people and pointing them toward righteousness. Islam acknowledges the family as the essential social unit. A strong family is believed to be constructed on the foundation of the marriage between a husband and wife. Thanks to this bond, children are raised with affection, tenderness, and a sense of responsibility.

Islam places a high priority on maintaining family unity. Interestingly, the Arabic word for family, usra, is formed from terms that mean unity, cohesion, and protection. Muslims are often reminded, for the same reason, to maintain links within their blood family by the verses of the Quran and the Seerah of our beloved Prophet (PBUH).

Adam and Havaa, peace be upon them, were the first humans, and it was from them that the rest of humanity derived the concept of family. The Quran states:

> "O men, fear your Lord who created you from a single soul, and from it created its match, and spread many men and women from the two. Fear Allah (SWT) in whose name you ask each other (for your rights), and fear (the violation of the rights of) the womb-relations. Surely, Allah (SWT) is watchful over you." (Quran 4:1)

There are immaterial rewards for believers who devote time and energy to deepening their familial bonds. Numerous allusions in the Quran and Sunnah encourage us to preserve strong bonds with family members and believe our efforts will be repaid. The Prophet Muhammad (PBUH) is reported by Hazrat Anas (RA) to have said:

> *"Anyone who is pleased that his sustenance is expanded and his age extended should do kindness to his near relatives." (Sunah Abi Dawud)*

It is said that good deeds strengthen a believer's faith and that treating family members properly and helping them will result in Allah's (SWT) bounties, such as sustenance or rizq. This may manifest as either provision or health or as both.

> *"Your Lord has decreed that you worship none but Him, and do good to parents. If any one of them or both of them reach old age, do not say to them: uff (a word or expression of anger or contempt) and do not scold them, and address them with respectful words, and submit yourself before them in humility out of compassion, and say, 'My Lord, be merciful to them as they have brought me up in my childhood.'" (Quran 17:23-24)*

Even if one comes from among the non-believers, one still has a duty to maintain family connections and treat their parents with kindness, duty, and respect. The command to treat parents kindly follows the need to obey Allah (SWT) in multiple places in the Quran and Sunnah. Its placement highlights how important it is. Furthermore, we naturally establish an example for our kids to follow into the next generation by treating our parents with duty and respect.

Maintaining relationships with extended family and relatives is very important in Islam. Family support or love is one of the essential pillars in a person's life, building a great aspect for an individual staying in a marital relationship. It is, therefore, essential to strike a balance between all the formal family relationships as well as obligations during marital life if there is going to be harmony within the household. Following the prophetic directives, couples should draw closer and achieve unity within themselves and perhaps the rest of their extended family members.

Balancing Family Relationships and Obligations with Marital Life

Balancing family relationships with marital life is one of the hardest but essentially vital ways of nurturing a healthy family environment. The couple needs to understand that, even though the primary commitment is between them, relationships between them and their extended family members add richness to their lives and bolster their general welfare.

To strike this balance, couples must discuss their expectations and boundaries regarding family involvement and ensure they both feel comfortable with the engagements. Approaching family responsibilities should be a joint effort; a couple should decide together what may be shared values and priorities. Such teamwork strengthens the bonding within the relationship and creates a sense of unity in managing the extended family relationships.

Boundaries protect the marital space while ensuring both carry their responsibilities toward extended family members. This requires setting certain moments for family gatherings or limiting those interactions that may bring conflict. Communication of boundaries should not lead to misplacement and should allow the couple to change their relations with their relatives.

More importantly, couples must understand that family responsibilities carry different weights depending on the culture and personal values of the family. Respecting each other's family customs and traditions is very important in building compassion and helping navigate the multigenerational complexity. Celebrating milestones, attending gatherings, and providing support during tough times honour these relationships while keeping the marital bond healthy.

Prophetic Guidance on Fostering Unity and Harmony Within the Extended Family

As the Prophet Muhammad (PBUH) himself said, family ties, which extend to every member of the extended family, are not to be separated but treated with kindness, respect, and generosity. Among the important teachings of the Prophet (PBUH) is that looking after close and distant relatives is righteous.

The Prophet (PBUH) encouraged interdependence among family members in times of crisis and times of celebration. Acts of kindness and support bring love together with unity, helping to strengthen bonds within the family through community relationships.

Families work toward a greater goal of unity by having regular gatherings, sharing meals, and participating in social activities. It helps to strengthen these loving and mutual relationships.

Furthermore, the Prophet (PBUH) emphasised the importance of forgiveness and reconciliation within families. Conflicts may arise, but it is essential to approach these situations with a spirit of understanding and compassion.

The Quran encourages believers to "make peace between your brothers" (Quran 49:10), reminding individuals of the importance of resolving disputes and fostering harmony.

The act of visiting relatives, especially those who may be ill or in need, is also a significant practice encouraged by the Prophet (PBUH) he stated,

"Visit the sick, feed the hungry, and free the captive."
(Sahih Muslim)

This guidance reinforces the idea that maintaining ties with relatives is not only a social obligation but also a means of earning Allah's (SWT) pleasure.

This balance between maintaining ties with extended family and relatives with marital responsibilities is a vital aspect of Islamic life; only through such a balance can a couple maintain a happy family environment. Couples can strengthen their marriage and advance relationships with their relatives by maintaining open communication, setting boundaries and making overall family dynamics a good teamwork exercise.

The prophetic advice concerning the theme of kindness, support, and forgiveness should remind them of the importance of unity among distant family members. Ultimately, a firm network support of the family will enrich the marital experience and foster a fulfilling and balanced life.

Chapter Eleven

Resolving Marital Issues: Seeking Guidance from Islam

Steps to Resolve Conflicts and Disagreements in Marriage

C onflicts are part and parcel of any relationship, including marriage. One of those "make-you-or-break-you" situations is marital strife. Allah (SWT) made this partnership, which is bound for
conflict, for a reason. A marriage might be utterly destroyed by marital strife and forced into an agonising divorce. Alternatively, it can
strengthen a couple's relationship to the point that they taste something delicious, akin to a hint of Jannah, the Garden of Paradise.

Any close connection will inevitably experience conflict. Two people
cannot be emotionally close if they do not have any innate differences
that cause them to feel anxious. This feeling of trepidation is accompanied by storms of fear, wrath, frustration, and disappointment, all of
which are perfectly normal.

On a personal level, marriage discord can delay personal growth and
self-improvement. Many couples forget that disagreements don't have

to become the primary source of tension unless they allow it to. People are not helpless victims of their own emotions, doomed to quarrel and fight over feelings beyond their control.

Yet, unlike conflicts with friends or relatives, disagreements with a spouse – someone you live with daily – can completely destroy your marriage. You want a close, lasting relationship with them, but love love doesn't mean tolerating everything.

Differing from your spouse can also serve as a bit of a reality check, as it forces you to acknowledge that just because you were raised with a particular belief or way of thinking doesn't mean it's correct. There may be some merit to certain disagreements. However, this tends to make some people feel extremely insecure. These distinctions may be concerning politics, religion, family, upbringing, culture, intimacy, or even something as minor as favourite foods or activities.

Above all, dealing with conflict is an opportunity to grow and accept some of your flaws. That, then, is the ladder to adulthood. And that's what a marriage consists of: two people who both owe it to the other to be the greatest and most mature versions of them.

Wives and husbands aren't always meant to agree on everything. That isn't feasible. Since marital conflict usually involves two people, whether we like to admit it or not, it is truly an opportunity to see how you, and not the other, have been participating in some continuing issue in your marriage. The good news is that we have the instant and enormous capacity to make a positive change just by altering our own behaviour because, in marriage, it always takes two.

Resolution based on understanding respect and compassion is important for a healthy marital relationship in Islam. Disagreements are to be dealt with constructively, as taught in the Quran and the Sunnah. Couples can resolve conflicts and strengthen their bond by adopting Islamic dispute resolution methods or seeking guidance when necessary.

The fundamental approach to managing these emotional interaction issues is in a situation like this: first, we should stop focusing so much on our partner and instead begin a regular self-evaluation of our actions. We should always examine our own behaviour before trying to correct a partner for whatever they may be doing that we think is wrong.

Even if we believe our partner is acting inappropriately, we have typically unknowingly supported and even facilitated such behaviour. The sole individual you can change when it comes to confrontation is yourself. So, changing your personal role in a harmful behaviour pattern with your spouse is the first step towards treating marital conflict.

Put another way, even as hard as we may to change our husbands' undesirable behaviour, we often encourage it. By being careless with his schedule, the spouse who believes his wife only wants to control him is fuelling her craving for power. The nag-then-punish mentality of the resentful wife of a lethargic husband encourages resistance from him.

Whenever you feel like blaming your partner for something, you should stop, step back, and examine yourself honestly. Are things actually the way you see them? Is she genuinely just being bossy? Is he truly that indolent? Are these basic flaws in your partner's character, or are they a response to a more complicated issue you both contribute to?

Islamic Modes of Conflict Resolution and Seeking a Mediator

Islam teaches positive and respectful methods of conflict resolution. Both parties should take time to listen to one another's thoughts without interruption or belittling feelings. Active listening helps promote the understanding and sympathy of both characters and lets them feel heard and valued.

When conflicts arise, it is important to approach them to find a solution rather than winning an argument.

The Quran emphasises the importance of reconciliation in "And if two factions among the believers should fight, then make settlement between the two." (Quran 49:9)

This verse highlights the significance of striving for peace and resolution rather than allowing disagreements to escalate.

Communication is crucial in any marriage, but it goes beyond simply expressing your feelings. People have a distinct communication style that shapes how they express themselves and perceive others. Acknowledging and comprehending your spouse's communication style is essential to creating a successful Muslim marriage.

Effective communication is essential to a thriving Muslim marriage. It entails speaking positively and sending encouraging messages that deepen the emotional connection between partners. Emphasising good communication may create a more caring and encouraging atmosphere in your marriage, making it simpler to overcome obstacles when they arise.

Using "I" sentences is one of the best strategies for practising constructive communication. Try utilising words like "I feel" or "I think" to express your ideas and feelings with your partner rather than placing blame or making accusations. This strategy can assist in averting possible confrontations and fostering more sympathetic and cooperative partnerships.

There are no mind readers! Our spouse won't know our innermost thoughts and feelings if we don't communicate them. Many of us believe that since our spouse is the one who knows us the best, they should be able to tell why we are angry or frustrated without us having to express it, which can cause misunderstandings and even more frustration. If you don't talk to your spouse and share your views, they won't know what's on your mind.

Start sharing everything with your partner instead of assuming they will understand you. Do not hesitate to share a story, even if you don't find it hilarious. It's time to start talking about everything that's going on in your life. Talk about your day, your experiences, and all of your thoughts, both happy and sad. Your relationship will strengthen, and your mutual understanding will deepen as a result.

When speaking with your spouse, focusing entirely on them is critical because it makes them feel listened to and important. Thus, when spending time with each other, put your laptop, mobile phone, or other distractions aside.

Using social media or texting someone while conversing is rather popular these days; it gives your spouse the feeling that there are more important people for you to be talking to. This is seen as typical multitasking. Problems might occasionally occur when your partner is talking about something important or depressing, and you find yourself giggling because of a social media post, making them feel unheard.

Your spouse anticipates understanding you in the same way that you do. Even if it isn't relevant, pay attention to what they experienced and how they spent their day. This will inspire them to share things with you, enhancing mutual comprehension and communication.

Expressing to your partner that you appreciate them is another approach to engaging in positive communication. Try your hardest to thank them for their contributions and show them how much you care. Saying "thank you" or "I appreciate you" are simple yet powerful ways to establish a closer emotional bond.

Lastly, paying attention to your body language and tone of voice is critical. A negative tone or gesture might contradict your words and send a whole different message, even if you're trying to promote positivity. As you communicate with your spouse, remember to keep an open mind and a cheerful disposition. Engaging in constructive conversation can foster a loving and supportive atmosphere in your Muslim marriage and ultimately improve your emotional bond.

Good communication is necessary for a Muslim marriage to succeed. It's important for creating a solid and healthy marriage bond between partners. Couples can overcome communication obstacles and establish a stronger connection by being aware of each other's communication preferences, actively listening, speaking positively, and utilising the right technology.

Putting money into good communication is essential to creating a happy Muslim marriage. Although it requires time and work, the benefits are substantial. One very good step if direct communication fails is to consider mediation.

Mediation in Islam includes the introduction of a neutral third party who can represent you and discuss the matter with your spouse to bring the discussion to the point where you or your spouse reaches a solution you can mutually agree on. This mediator can be your trusted member of the family, a friend, or a community leader who knows the principles of Islam and can guide you accordingly.

In mediation, there must be an agreement between both parties to select a mediator and seek the process with an ear to listen and compromise. The mediator's role is to make the setting safe for the parties to express their feelings and concerns without judgment.

Seeking Guidance from Religious Scholars and Marriage Counselors

Some conflicts require the insight of a mature mind, like that of a religious scholar or a marriage counsellor. Experts can give illuminating insights from religious teachings, and such a couple will be able to resolve their problems with a better understanding of their faith.

A couple seeking advice from a religious scholar should choose someone who is learned and held in high regards in the community. They can then allow scholars to give them advice based on the Quranic teachings and the Hadith, which will find them solutions to the tenets of Islam. They can both remind their partners about their responsibilities to one another and the importance of being patient and understanding in marriage.

Marriage counsellors may help Islamic principles because they have more profound concerns and thus cause conflicts. Counsellors can offer a lot of practical strategies for communication and solving conflict besides providing emotional support. It may also make sessions about both partners so they can express their feelings and develop skills in dealing with disagreement.

Thus, these couples are advised to first seek leadership and wisdom in resolving their conflicts by praying for God's direction and enlightenment. Looking unto Allah (SWT) in prayer strengthens the couple's bond with their Creator and brings an atmosphere of cooperation and understanding into their approaches toward reconciliation.

Conflicts and differences between spouses in the marriage need commitment, understanding, and compassion. Islamic ways to resolve conflict include open communication and mediation. Couples can come together to solve their differences constructively. There is nothing wrong with seeking advice from religious scholars or marriage counsellors who improve their competencies further to tackle arguments.

All this brings a positive influence on the marital bond if reconciliation and unity are strengthened more as per kind and mutual respect within the principles of Islam.

Importance of Reliance on Allah (SWT) During Marital Challenges

Marriage, a sacred union in Islam, is not without its challenges. Navigating the complexities of a relationship requires effort, understanding, and, above all, the virtues of patience, prayer, and reliance on Allah (SWT). During times of marital difficulties, these elements become crucial for sustaining the bond between spouses and finding resolution. Emphasising these practices helps individuals cultivate a spirit of resilience and hope, reinforcing their commitment to each other and their faith.

The Role of Patience in Marriage

Patience, or sabr, is a fundamental virtue in Islam that plays a vital role in overcoming marital challenges. The Quran frequently highlights the importance of patience, encouraging believers to persevere through trials with grace and humility.

> *Allah (SWT) states, "Indeed, Allah (SWT) is with the patient." (Quran 2:153)*

This assurance emphasises that enduring hardships, including those faced in marriage, bring divine support and guidance.

In times of conflict, patience allows couples to respond thoughtfully rather than react impulsively. By exercising restraint and refraining from harsh words or actions, partners can create a conducive environment for resolving disagreements.

Patience fosters emotional stability, enabling individuals to approach issues with clarity and a willingness to understand each other's perspectives.

Moreover, practising patience cultivates empathy and compassion within the marriage. When partners strive to understand each other's feelings and struggles, it strengthens their bond and helps them navigate difficulties together. This sense of shared resilience transforms challenges into opportunities for growth, reinforcing the idea that enduring hardships together are part of the marital journey.

The Power of Prayer

In addition to patience, prayer is a powerful tool for seeking solace and guidance during marital challenges. Turning to Allah (SWT) in prayer strengthens the connection between spouses and their Creator. The Prophet Muhammad (PBUH) taught that sincere supplication can bring change and healing in one's life.

Prophetic supplications and prayers, such as Dua for marital harmony, serve as a means of seeking divine assistance in resolving conflicts and restoring peace. For instance, one can recite the following supplication: "O Allah (SWT), unite our hearts, make us love each other, and grant us mutual understanding." Such prayers express a longing for harmony and reinforce the couple's commitment to relying on Allah's (SWT) wisdom and mercy.

The act of praying together can further strengthen the marital bond. Couples who engage in joint prayer cultivate a sense of unity and shared purpose. This practice fosters a spiritual connection, reminding them of their collective reliance on Allah (SWT) and their mutual commitment to navigate challenges together.

Strengthening Faith and Spirituality

In relation to marital problems, faith and spirituality should also be increased. Among the acts of worship that might bring peace and clarity to the heart include the recitation of the Quran, the performance of Salah, and remembrance of Allah (SWT) in dhikr. These are all reminders that there is a bigger purpose for marriage to happen and that marital responsibilities are significant and important to be maintained.

Whenever there is a crisis, couples need to reflect on the interpretations of the Quran and the Sunnah on compassion, forgiveness, and understanding. This is how the environment they give each other can be nurturing, encouraging healing and reconciliation.

Besides, the knowledge of Islam's teachings regarding marriage can also rejuvenate a couple so that they can face their problems wisely. The Quran and Hadith mention the rights and obligations of the spouses, which can be used as the basis for solving conflicts between them. It brings accountability to partners, forcing them to fulfil these commitments they made with each other.

In marriage, love alone cannot always sustain patience, especially during challenging times. When couples face marital struggles, patience, prayer, and reliance on Allah (SWT) are needed to build a resilient and fulfilling relationship. With grown patience and actually praying, the couple need not react selfishly or blindly to sit for negotiation of their conflicts. Worship and learning enhance faith and spirituality and bring the couple close to each other and Allah (SWT). Ultimately, these virtues guide the couples through the trials of marriage, strengthening their bond further and reinforcing their faith in the divine.

Chapter Twelve

Conclusion

In conclusion, it would be achievable for any couple committed to following Islamic principles to build a loving and lasting marriage based on Sunnah guidance. This is a means whereby couples will prosper in love, mercy, and mutual respect within their marital bond by practically instilling their relationship with the teachings of the Quran and the examples of Prophet Muhammad (PBUH). This book has covered the various sides of the Islamic marriage institution, which involves preparing to marry with sincerity and intention, then sets about ascertaining the rights and responsibilities between both spouses, and still resolving conflicts patiently and in faith.

One needs to take an appropriate approach to the bond of marriage, for it is the base of tranquillity and friendship for human beings and spiritual growth in Islam. Understanding, compassion, and a willingness to compromise are essential elements for gaining success in marriage. One must constantly seek Allah's (SWT) guidance and strengthen the relationship between couples with acts of kindness and love by keeping their communication open.

Blessed is the marriage of those couples and families that fulfil the Sunnah and try to follow the principles of love, compassion, and cooperation in their married life. The path to a successful and fulfilling marriage is long, but Allah's (SWT) guidance and the wisdom of Islamic teachings can lead to real happiness and contentment in this world and the Hereafter.

Find Out More

Website: www.barakahinbusiness.com

Socials: @barakahinbusiness

If you enjoyed this book, kindly leave a review to help expand our reach so others may benefit also.